INDIAN CURRIES

A varied selection of appetizing and easily made dishes
including breads, *dhalls*, pilaus, relishes and unusual curries
with nutritious vegetarian ingredients.

INDIAN CURRIES

by

HARVEY DAY

Illustrated by Clive Birch

THORSONS PUBLISHERS LIMITED
Wellingborough, Northamptonshire

First published 1982
Second Impression 1983

British Library Cataloguing in Publication Data

Day, Harvey
    Indian curries.
    1. Cookery, India
    I. Title
    641.5954   TX724.5.14

    ISBN 0-7225-0781-X

Printed in Great Britain by
Richard Clay (The Chaucer Press) Ltd,
Bungay, Suffolk

CONTENTS

INTRODUCTION

There are no hard and fast rules about preparing curries, which vary with the part of the country in which they are made and with the preferences of those who concoct them. In North India they are, generally speaking, much milder than in the South, and the ingredients for the same sort of curry may also vary with the location.

The beginner would be well advised to use less chilli than the amount given in the recipes; if not pungent enough, extra chilli can be added to the curry at the next attempt. If preferred, use less fat and salt than the stated quantities; with non-stick pans very little fat is needed and such curries may be enjoyed by the keenest slimmer. If you have never made curries, attempt the simpler ones first; these include Cauliflower Curry, Shredded Cabbage, *Khichiri, Dhall Churchurree* and *Poorees. Samosas* and *Kachowries* are also easy to make and very tasty; nor is there any need to use all the spices mentioned.

Spices may be bought by the pound and these can be expensive; 4 oz (100g) of any spice does go a long way, however, as only small quantities are used in any recipe. If stored in air-tight jars, away from the light, they seem to improve with keeping. The Curry Club spices can be used as they are, need neither grinding nor roasting and are cheaper than those sold in the shops.

Indian names may be confusing. *Dhall* may be spelt *dal*, *poorees* are also known as *puris* and *bhajees* as *bhajis*. The same food may be known by different names in different parts of the country:

for instance, *sambals, bhurtas* and *raitas* all have much in common.

When you have learnt how to make them, curries take less time to prepare and cook than most European dishes. If you like curries, you may tend to eat them almost every day – don't! Space them out – serve them once a week or once a month – and this way you will enjoy them more.

Spices For Health

All curry spices, if used in moderation, promote health and stimulate the appetite. Here is a list of the most common, together with their Hindi names, which will help when buying ingredients from Indian food shops.

Allspice (seetul). This is often used instead of cinnamon and is aromatic and antiseptic.

Aniseed (souf or *sonf)*. This is well known for its digestive properties. In Britain, it is used in sweets and cakes; in India, the roasted seeds are put into *paan*, which is chewed after a meal to aid digestion and prevent flatulence.

Asafoetida (hing). This is one of the spices used in making curries.

Black pepper (kala mirchi). This creates bodily heat and is antiseptic; together with other ingredients, it is administered by *kavirajes** in cases of fever. The whole peppercorns, but not the powder, are used to flavour some curries; it is also a heart stimulant.

Cardamom (eelachie). The seeds are used in curries and in sweets; it is antiseptic, with a powerful perfumed flavour.

Chillies (mirchi). These are used fresh and in powder form to give curries their pungency. Fresh green chillies are even more pungent than red; in small quantities, they are a heart stimulant.

Cinnamon (dalchini). This acts as a more powerful germicide than carbolic acid! It is used in curries, sweets and cakes.

* Practitioners of *Ayurvedic* medicine.

Cloves (laoong). These are an even more powerful antiseptic than cinnamon; powdered cloves are used in many curries and some sweets.

Coriander (dhunnia). This is an antiseptic and carminative.

Cummin (jeera). Both powder and seeds are used in curries and impart the most powerful of all flavours, so must be used circumspectly.

Fenugreek (meythi). The seeds are used for flavouring, mainly in pickles and vegetable curries; it is one of the ingredients of *panch phora* (see page 14).

Garlic (lassoon). This is a powerful germicide and blood cleanser, rich in vitamins B, C and D, and in sulphur, which makes the breath offensive (although this does not occur when garlic is cooked). It is used widely in almost all curries. Garlic is a natural antibiotic and is valuable in the treatment of high blood pressure; it is also an aid in the cure of TB.

Ginger, dry (sont). This is used in cooking.

Ginger, fresh (udruk). Fresh ginger is preferable to dry or powdered ginger and is used in curries, pickles and chutneys. The root has been used medicinally in Britain since 1597 and, according to recent research published in *The Lancet*, it acts as a specific against motion sickness.

Mace (jawatrie). This is the outer skin of the nutmeg and is used for flavouring dishes such as *pilaus.*

Mustard seed (rai). The mustard seeds are used in curries and to make a paste for pickles; in Bengal in particular, mustard oil is used in cooking and for massaging the skin; it is rich in vitamin D, has about 98 per cent fat and contains traces of manganese, nickel and cobalt.

Nutmeg (jauphull). This is used in powdered form for flavouring, although freshly grated nutmeg is preferable to powdered nutmeg. It should not be used in excessive quantities, since it can act as a drug.

Poppy seeds (khus khus). These are used in some *garam massalas* and sweetmeats, and may be sprinkled on breads.

Turmeric (huldi). This is a root plant of the ginger family, which gives curries their yellow colour. It is also used instead of the more expensive saffron in preparing yellow rice and some pilaus. A little of this spice goes a long way. In India, the root pulverized, is always used in preference to the powder.

Curry Powders
The main ingredients of the following curry powders may be varied or omitted according to the flavours you prefer. The following recipes can be made up and stored in air-tight jars or bottles, in which they will keep indefinitely; in fact, their flavour will improve with keeping.

To make any of the curry powders, lightly grill the spices such as coriander, red chilli, cummin, fenugreek, peppercorns and mustard seed, then discard any husks. Curry leaves must be dried, then pounded and mixed with the other spices. All the spices should be pounded, sifted through muslin and mixed together. Garlic and onions should be crushed and pounded and then mixed into the spice powder.

1. 1 lb (½ kilo) coriander seeds   5 oz (150g) dried chillies
    5 oz (150g) turmeric   3 oz (75g) fenugreek seeds
    3 oz (75g) black peppercorns   2½ oz (65g) mustard seeds
    2½ oz (65g) cummin seeds   4 oz (100g) garlic
    ½ oz (15g) cardamom   2½ oz (65g) curry leaves
    1 oz (25g) sea salt   2 oz (50g) raw cane sugar

2. 1 lb (½ kilo) coriander seeds   2 oz (50g) dried red chillies
    3 oz (75g) cummin seeds   2 oz (50g) fenugreek seeds
    2 oz (50g) black peppercorns   2 oz (50g) mustard seeds
    2 oz (50g) garlic   1 oz (25g) sea salt
    1 oz (25g) curry leaves

3. 1 lb (½ kilo) coriander seeds 2 oz (50g) dried red chillies
    2 oz (50g) turmeric 4 oz (100g) fenugreek seeds
    2 oz (50g) peppercorns 2 oz (50g) mustard seeds
    4 oz (100g) cummin seeds 2 oz (50g) garlic
    1½ teaspoonsful cardamom 1½ oz (40g) cinnamon
    4 oz (100g) curry leaves 2 oz (50g) dried ginger
    ½ lb (¼ kilo) poppy seeds 1 oz (25g) sea salt

4. 1¼ lb (600g) coriander seeds ½ lb (¼ kilo) dried red chillies
    3 oz (75g) turmeric 1 oz (25g) fenugreek seeds
    2 oz (50g) peppercorns 2 oz (50g) mustard seeds
    3 oz (75g) curry leaves 2 oz (50g) cummin seeds
    3 oz (75g) garlic 1 oz (25g) sea salt

Note: This curry powder is hot.

5. 1 lb (½ kilo) coriander seeds ¾ lb (350g) dried red chillies
    3 oz (75g) turmeric 1 oz (25g) fenugreek seeds
    2 oz (50g) peppercorns 2 oz (50g) mustard seeds
    3 oz (75g) curry leaves 2 oz (50g) cummin seeds
    3 oz (75g) garlic 1 oz (25g) sea salt

Note: This curry powder is very hot.

6. 1 lb (½ kilo) coriander seeds 1 lb (½ kilo) dried red chillies
    6 oz (175g) turmeric 4 oz (100g) fenugreek seeds
    2 oz (50g) peppercorns 4 oz (100g) mustard seeds
    ¾ lb (350g) cummin seeds 1 oz (25g) curry leaves
    1 oz (25g) sea salt

Note: This curry powder is very hot.

7. 1 lb (½ kilo) coriander seeds
    6 oz (175g) turmeric
    4 oz (100g) mustard seeds
    ½ lb (¼ kilo) garlic
    2 oz (50g) cinnamon
    1 oz (25g) sea salt

    1 lb (½ kilo) dried red chillies
    2 oz (50g) peppercorns
    ½ lb (¼ kilo) cummin seeds
    2 oz (50g) cardamom
    2 oz (50g) curry leaves

Note: This curry powder is very hot.

8. 1 lb (½ kilo) coriander seeds
    2 oz (50g) turmeric
    1½ oz (40g) peppercorns
    5 oz (150g) cummin seeds
    2 oz (50g) curry leaves

    ¾ lb (350g) dried red chillies
    3 oz (75g) fenugreek seeds
    2½ oz (65g) mustard seeds
    6 oz (175g) garlic
    1 oz (25g) sea salt

Note: This curry powder is very hot.

9. 1 lb (½ kilo) coriander seeds
    5 oz (150g) turmeric
    2½ oz (65g) peppercorns
    4 oz (100g) cummin seeds
    1 oz (25g) cardamom
    1 oz (25g) cloves
    2 oz (50g) curry leaves

    ½ lb (¼ kilo) dried red chillies
    2 oz (50g) fenugreek seeds
    2½ oz (65g) mustard seeds
    2½ oz (65g) garlic
    1 oz (25g) cinnamon
    1 teacupful coriander leaves
    1 oz (25g) sea salt

Note: This curry powder is hot.

10. 1 lb (½ kilo) coriander seeds
    2 oz (50g) turmeric
    2 oz (50g) peppercorns
    2 oz (50g) curry leaves

    4 oz (100g) dried red chillies
    1 oz (25g) cummin seeds
    1 oz (25g) mustard seeds
    2 teaspoonsful sea salt

Curry Paste (Hot)

1 lb (½ kilo) coriander seeds
5 oz (150g) turmeric
2½ oz (65g) peppercorns
2 oz (50g) garlic
1 oz (25g) cinnamon
1 teacupful coriander leaves
4 onions
1 pint (½ litre) cider vinegar
1½ oz (40g) sea salt
½ lb (¼ kilo) ghee or vegetable fat

½ lb (¼ kilo) dried red chillies
2 oz (50g) fenugreek seeds
2½ oz (65g) mustard seeds
1 oz (25g) cardamom
1 oz (25g) cloves
6 oz (175g) tamarind
1 coconut
¾ pint (400ml) white wine vinegar

To make this paste, pound all the spices finely and pass them through a muslin sieve. Onions, garlic and coriander leaves should be ground and rubbed into the curry powder between the palms of the hands.

The pulp of the tamarind and the milk of the coconut must be mixed with the vinegar and passed through a sieve. Mix together the spices, coconut and tamarind extract, add the coriander leaves and salt and fry in the heated fat for 5 minutes. Bottle, when cool, in air-tight jars and use as much as you need from day to day.

Garam Massala

Literally, this means 'hot spices', though one particular British firm sells *garam massala* which lacks even a trace of pungency. You can concoct your own combinations and find which you like best. Some standard recipes are: cummin seeds, cinnamon and cloves; peppercorns, coriander seeds and fennel seeds; fennel, cloves and cardamom; whole cummin, cummin seeds and crushed red chillies; cloves, cinnamon, ground coriander, ginger, nutmeg and ground cummin.

*The Curry Club Recipe**
The Curry Club gives an excellent recipe for *garam massala:*

4 oz (100g) coriander seeds	1 oz (25g) cardamom
4 oz (100g) cummin seeds	½ oz (15g) grated nutmeg
2 oz (50g) black peppercorns	½ oz (15g) ginger powder
1 oz (25g) cassia bark	A few bay leaves
1 oz (25g) cloves	

It is possible to buy this combination of spices, ready-mixed from the Curry Club, and all you have to do is use the *garam massala* as you would curry powder.

Many Indian and Pakistani shops sell their own *garam massala* made up to the proprietors' recipes, and these vary according to tastes and the part of the country from which they originate. The ready-made variety is a short cut and saves much time in weighing, mixing, roasting and grinding.

It is better, however, to make your own *garam massala*; if you like one spice more than another, you can add extra, or if you dislike a particular spice, leave it out. Incidentally, white pepper is never used in curries. Where ground pepper is used, mill your own black peppercorns. (After grinding the spices in a coffee mill, always grind some hard or toasted wholemeal bread crusts to remove the lingering smell of spices, otherwise your coffee might taste of them too!)

* The address of the Curry Club is: Pat Chapman, The Curry Club, P.O. Box 7, Haslemere, Surrey GU27 1EP.

Panch Phora
In India, curry spices such as turmeric, cummin, coriander and ginger are pounded on a large, flat, pitted stone called a *seel*, where they are mixed with water or vinegar and made into a paste. In this way, all the essential ingredients and the true flavour are retained. Curry powders are, of course, heated, and thereby lose some of their flavour. In *panch phora*, the essence of the seeds is retained as they are added whole.

Panch means five, and it is a corruption of this word which is used for 'punch', to describe an alcoholic drink consisting of brandy, gin, rum, whisky and tea.

The two most popular kinds of *panch phora* are: mustard seed, aniseed, cummin, cassia leaves and red chilli; and cummin, fenugreek, aniseed, mustard seed and black cummin. Some stores sell *panch phora* in quarter, half and one pound packets. It needs no preparation; all you have to do is to sprinkle a teaspoonful into a casserole of vegetables, mix it in and these seeds will impart a flavour different from anything you have ever tasted. The amount can always be increased, but do not add too much at first.

Saffron

Saffron *(Crocus sativa)* was given in nearly all the original recipes but as the cost today is prohibitive (½g for 50p), turmeric is used as a substitute. Turmeric is not quite as delicate and lacks the aroma of saffron but it is within the financial reach of all. Saffron is made from the dried stigmatas of the saffron flower. As it has to be picked by hand and from 60,000-70,000 by dried weight yield only 1 lb of saffron, labour costs have made it an unprofitable crop. For three centuries it used to be cultivated in Saffron Walden, which took its name from the flower. Originally the town was Chipping Walden. The Indian name for saffron is *kesha.*

Chillies

The most misused of all spices is the chilli, which gives curries their pungency; unfortunately, the mistaken idea exists that no curry is worthy of the name unless it takes the skin of your tongue, brings tears to your eyes and sweat to your forehead! There are those who like their curries burning hot, and those who do not. Indeed, curries need have no chilli in them at all. I like to bring out the full flavour of the spices, so the curries I make contain little chilli or none at all. If you see a recipe that mentions ½oz (15g) of chilli, try using ¼oz (7g) to start with;

you can always increase the quantity when you next cook, but as with salt, you cannot remove chilli. (Incidentally, fresh green chillies are more pungent than the dried red variety; their pungency lies mainly in the seeds).

Rice
Rice is the great filler of the East and in India it is eaten at every main meal, except where *chapattis* or *parathas* are served. Many people in Britain, brought up in the rice-and-prunes or soggy rice tradition, look with suspicion on this cereal unless they have been taught to cook it properly or are given recipes of easily made dishes. This is essential because stodgy, sticky rice can be an unappetizing mess. Cooked as it should be, rice is always palatable.

Rice may be eaten with all curries, with the accompaniment of only pickles, or with *dhall* (lentils). Many people claim that rice is fattening and full of starch. This is not necessarily so as the starch is boiled into the water and, if this is drained off, only the cellulose remains, which is a form of roughage. There are two ways of preparing rice:

Plain Boiled Rice I
1. Almost fill a large pan with water and sprinkle in a cupful of brown rice, (which is sufficient for two people).

2. Bring the water to the boil, turn down the heat and simmer the rice for about 20 minutes, testing for softness after about 15 minutes.

3. When the grains are cooked through but still firm, remove the pan from the heat, place it in the sink and allow cold water to run into the rice. (This separates the grains.)

4. Pour off some of the liquid and add more cold water, then drain off all the water and empty the rice into a large, flat, ovenproof dish. Fluff up the rice with a fork to let out the steam and place the dish in a warm – not hot – oven, with the door ajar. (Leave for 5 or 10 minutes before serving.)

Note: In India, the rice water is not wasted; it is used, especially in South India, for making delicious sweets.

Plain Boiled Rice II

1. Measure out twice the volume of water to brown rice. Place the rice and water in a pan with a thick bottom and close-fitting lid and leave the rice to soak for 1 hour.

2. Bring the rice and water to the boil, lower the heat and simmer gently until all the water has been absorbed. (If this method is followed to the letter, the rice should be cooked through – but still firm – and ready to serve. Each grain should be separate when the last drop of water has evaporated.)

Note: This method is not as fool-proof as the first, for if there is too much water the rice is apt to be overcooked and the grains may stick to each other. It is well worth trying, however, because in this way none of the nutriment is lost, whilst in pouring off the water you drain away the starch as well.

Lentils

The little red lentils one sees in the shops are the most common variety of this legume, but many other varieties are also available and form the main protein food of hundreds of millions in India and the Far East. Until recently, lentils were used in Britain to make pease pudding and as thickeners in soups. Few people considered them as rivals to meat, fish, eggs and cheese.

Nowhere in the world have lentils made a more valuable contribution to human health than in India and Pakistan where they are the basis of a variety of dishes not known in the West until recently. These are known as *dhalls, dhals* or *dals*. Split peas are also called *dhalls*, as are whole, dried peas ('grams'), for all belong to the family *Leguminosae*.

Unleavened Bread

Bread was not made with yeast until the advent of the foreigners from the West: the Portuguese, the Dutch, the French and the British.

Throughout the Middle East, India and the Far East, unleavened bread is the bread of the people, for it does not need an oven. While out camping, I have seen excellent meals being cooked on improvized ovens constructed of three bricks and heated by firewood. The Indians seem to be natural cooks; with the most primitive implements they can turn out meals tastier than many produced by those who boast kitchens costing thousands of pounds.

Cooking Fats

In most parts of India, north of the Deccan, ghee is used for cooking, though in Bengal and Bangladesh a good deal of mustard oil is used. This also makes the best pickles. In frying, the oil must be heated until it gives off a thin blue smoke, otherwise the ingredients will have a mustard oil flavour. In the south, where coconut palms grow in profusion, coconut oil is the favoured medium for cooking, though a fair amount of peanut oil is also used. Today, the shops in Britain sell a variety of cooking fats, of which sunflower and peanut oils, polyunsaturated margarine and butter are suitable for cooking curries. There is no particular oil or fat that is best; much depends on the taste of the person making the curry.

Ghee or Clarified Butter

To most Indians, ghee is the finest of all cooking fats. It may be bought in shops specializing in Indian food, although this is the most expensive way to buy it and, because of the cost it is rarely, if ever, used for restaurant food.

Ghee or clarified butter imparts a distinctive taste to food; it is particularly popular as a cooking fat since it is less likely to burn and spoil the flavour of ingredients cooked in it.

To make ghee, place 1lb (½ kilo) of butter in a saucepan

together with a few cloves or a couple of bay leaves. Butter contains water, so let it boil until the water evaporates and spoon off any froth that rises to the surface. Continue cooking until there is no more froth. When it has cooled but is still liquid, strain the ghee through muslin into an air-tight jar and store it in a cool place, preferably a refrigerator where, unlike butter, it will not deteriorate.

Clarifying rids the ghee of any salt in the butter. For every pound of butter, you will end up with ¾ lb (350g) of ghee. Try it and decide whether the expense is worth it.

Milk and Its Products
A great deal of milk is drunk in India and it is also used for making yogurt and sweets. Oddly enough, none is made into the kinds of cheese we have in Britain. The only Indian cheese I know of is made in the little town of Bandal, on the Hooghly. This is a pleasant, flat cream cheese, about five inches wide and two inches thick; it is available smoked and unsmoked.

Dahi or Yogurt
The most common way of making yogurt is to take any quantity of milk, simmer it down to half its volume, and when it has cooled to about 120°F (49°C), a 'starter' is added. This may consist of lime or lemon juice, a tamarind solution, whey, or some previously made *dahi*. A small quantity will do. The starter is added at night and the milk is then covered and left in a warm place such as an airing cupboard, a warm spot in the kitchen or even a hay box. A wide-mouthed Thermos flask also makes a suitable container. In the morning, you should have yogurt! This process can be repeated half a dozen times, using some of the old yogurt as a starter.

If milk is not boiled to half its volume, but a starter is introduced at about 120°F (49°C), the sort of yogurt sold in the shops is produced.

Whey is never thrown away; it is used in making dough, added to some curries and soups, and in summer it is diluted, sweetened with sugar or honey, and lime or lemon is added to make a cooling drink. Sometimes, the whey is fed to pigs which thrive on it.

If milk goes sour in the bottle, do not throw it away. Stand it in a saucepan and heat it; the solids will separate from the whey. Strain the milk through a muslin cloth and cottage cheese will be produced. Some people may object that such cheese is full of germs. So it is, but they are harmless – even beneficial – germs. According to experiments carried out by Drs Harry Seneca and José M. Rosell, the whey in yogurt has bactericidal properties which are able to kill the amoeba in dysentery within five minutes; doctors have also used it in the treatment of colitis, gastroenteritis, constipation and other diseases. Provided the vessels in which you keep the acid milk are sterilized, do not be afraid to use it.

Kheer

Milk may be boiled down until a viscous substance is obtained, known as *kheer*. Sometimes, rice is also boiled in this way with raw cane sugar or honey and a few cardamom seeds to make a delicious rice pudding. This may be eaten hot or cold, and is very different from the rice pudding most of us know. (Cardamom seeds make all the difference to this dish.)

Khoa

If unsweetened *kheer* is boiled until all the water has evaporated, the residue is known as *khoa*, used in making numerous sweetmeats. It is a tedious operation making *khoa* as the milk has to be stirred constantly to prevent it sticking to the pan. However, non-stick pans do alleviate this problem.

Chhana or Curd

There is no equivalent to *chhana* in English cuisine; the nearest product is curd. (It must not be confused with *chana*, which means 'gram', a kind of pea.) To make *chhana,* lime or lemon juice – 1 lemon to 1 pint (½ litre) of liquid – is poured onto boiling milk, which curdles into solid lumps. When strained, the milk residue is known as *chhana*. To complete the process, a piece of muslin is tied around the neck of a wide-mouthed receptacle and whey is sprinkled on the cloth. Then the remaining milk and a little more whey are poured over the cloth where the milk curdles layer by layer. The four corners of the cloth are then tied and the solids are immersed in a tub of water. After four or five hours the solids will expand. (1 pint (½ litre) of milk produces about 4 oz (100g) of *chhana*.)

Finally, a weight is placed on the bag of *chhana* and the water is completely pressed out. Two kinds of *chhana* are made; one that can be cut into pieces and fried, the other somewhat spongier, from which the best kinds of sweets are made.

Coconut Milk

Coconut milk is used in many curries and adds greatly to their flavour. To extract the milk from a fresh coconut, a hole is made and the juice is poured out. When coconuts are not available, the milk can be made from desiccated coconut, or from the flesh of coconuts from which the juice has already been poured off. It is difficult to grate the flesh from a coconut and a special scraper, *(narial-ka-khoornee)*, is available in some Indian food stores.

If desiccated coconut is your only source, pour 1 cupful of boiling water over 6 oz (175g) of coconut and set it aside for 1 hour or overnight if possible. Then mash the coconut with a wooden spoon until the liquid is thick and creamy. Strain the liquid into a jug or bowl, add boiling water to the remaining flesh, soak it for an hour or more, and repeat the process. This will produce thin coconut milk which, when strained, is also used in curries and sauces.

It is also possible to buy coconut cream in Indian food stores; this must be diluted with water before use.

Tamarind Pulp

The word 'tamarind', fruit of the *Tamarindus indica*, is derived from the Arabic *tamar-hindi*, that is 'date of India'. Neither physically nor in flavour does it bear the least resemblance to the date, the only thing in common being the colour. The fruit is contained in a pod which has between one and twelve seeds embedded in soft brown or reddish-black, extremely acid pulp which sets one's teeth on edge. Tamarind is used medicinally, as a relish, and in cooking it imparts a flavour unlike any other ingredient. It must be used sparingly, however, for a little goes a long way and too much can spoil any curry.

The quantity depends on individual taste, so start with a little and if you like it, more can be added in your next attempt. It may be bought either in the pod or in pulp form; if in the pod, cover with boiling water for half an hour, then press out the pulp. For a 1½ in. ball of tamarind, use ¼ pint (150ml) of boiling water. If tamarind is not available, use lemon or lime juice (preferably lemon which is more acid than lime).

Tamarind Sauce I

1 ball of tamarind (1½ in.)
1 teaspoonful Barbados sugar or jaggery
3 half-inch slices ginger, chopped
5 dried red chillies, chopped
4 cloves garlic, chopped
Seeds of 1 cardamom
Sea salt to taste

1. Extract as much tamarind juice as possible by mashing the tamarind, mixing it with a little cider vinegar or water and straining it through a muslin or a fine sieve.

2. Add the sugar or jaggery and the salt and mix well.

3. Stir in the chillies, garlic and cardamom seeds, cook for 3 minutes and serve.

Note: A little tamarind sauce goes a long way. It will not keep for more than a few days without refrigeration.

Tamarind Sauce II

1 cupful tamarind (ripe)
1 dozen thin slices green ginger
Sea salt to taste
2 dried red chillies, chopped
3 tablespoonsful cider vinegar
Raw cane sugar to taste

1. Boil the tamarind in 1 cupful of water.

2. Mix together the ginger and chillis with a little water and salt. Add the tamarind and mix again.

3. Simmer this mixture for a couple of minutes and, when cool, press the pulp through a fine sieve. Add sugar to taste.

Pepper Water

Some people, even in Britain, like their curries very hot and do not think they have sampled a 'real curry' unless beads of perspiration form on their foreheads and tears roll down their cheeks. For them, pepper water is the essential ingredient in a curry.

There are many recipes for pepper water, which is a South Indian concoction. People in the south of the country, nearest the equator, like their food very pungent because, one assumes, it makes them sweat and thereby cools their bodies. Here is the simplest recipe, although there are other and more deadly ones!

1 oz (25 g) tamarind pulp
1 teaspoonful cummin
2 cloves garlic, chopped
1 oz (25 g) vegetable fat
3 red chillies, ground
½ in. piece of turmeric root
2 onions, sliced
2-3 curry leaves

1. Mix the cummin, garlic, chilli and turmeric with the tamarind pulp.

2. Place the mixture in 1 cupful of water and boil it for 15 minutes. Allow the liquid to cool and then strain it through a fine sieve.

3. Fry the onions with the curry leaves in the fat.

4. Pour in the tamarind water, add salt to taste, and bring it to the boil, then remove the pan from the heat. Serve with plenty of rice.

Note: If any dish is so hot that it makes you gasp, do not reach for the jug of iced water. Plenty of plain boiled rice is the best antidote, and bread is the next best.

Sprouting Mung Beans

Beans are easily sprouted; mung beans are the best and have the highest protein and vitamin content. They are also the most easily sprouted, but are available, already sprouted, in some supermarkets.

Place 1 dessertspoonful of beans in a plastic container. Cover them with water and soak them overnight in a warm place. After 24 hours, rinse the beans in a sieve, replace them in the container, put on the lid and place them in an airing cupboard or warm spot. On the next day, the beans should start sprouting. Rinse them again and put them back in the container in a warm place. The beans should, by now, have sprouted to a length of 1½ in. and may be eaten raw in salads or cooked.

One advantage of sprouting your own beans is that they can be enjoyed all the year round, when fresh vegetables are scarce. If too many beans are sprouted, they can be kept in the refrigerator for a number of days.

Mangoes or Aam

In India, the mango is considered to be the king of fruits. There are many varieties, from the *laingra aam* and the Bombay *aam*, to the 'turpentine mango', which tastes as its name suggests!

Tinned mangoes are available in some supermarkets and all shops that specialize in Indian spices. Many people who have not sampled them are still suspicious, but now that there is a considerable tourist trade between Britain and India, there must be thousands who have enjoyed the mango in its natural habitat. In Britain, mango pulp can also be bought and this makes an excellent filling for tarts and pies.

The mango has been cultivated in India for hundreds of years and is mentioned in ancient Sanskrit literature. Today, this fruit is grown in South China, Malaysia, Indonesia, Madagascar, tropical Africa, Burma, Egypt, Persia, Brazil, the West Indies and the U.S.A. In India, five hundred varieties are available.

The flavour of the best mangoes is delicious, and they are also rich in fruit sugar. The mango is a good source of niacin and riboflavin and its vitamin C content is four times that of the apple. If eaten in sufficient quantities, it acts as a laxative, and in India the mango has, for centuries, been used as a cure for liver disorders and for convalescents who wish to put on weight. There is no Eastern fruit to compare with this one and the *Ayurveda* system of medicine recommends the eating of mangoes to aid growth, longevity and defective vision.

The unripe mango is used for making jam, chutney and pickle. It contains tartaric, malic, and a trace of citric acid as well as 4,800 iu's of vitamin A per 100g. When analyzed, the mango was found to contain 87.4 per cent water, 0.06 per cent protein, 0.4 per cent fat, 9.9 per cent carbohydrates, mainly in the form of sugar, and 0.5 per cent mineral matter, mainly potassium. Unripe mangoes are also used for curries as the flesh is firm and does not break up easily when cooked.

Rissole Nut Mix
The following recipes are used in several of the main curry dishes.

Rissole Nut Mix I

1 cupful ground walnuts
2 cupsful wholemeal breadcrumbs
2 eggs
Dash of freshly ground black pepper
1 onion, finely diced
1 teaspoonful *Marmite* or *Vecon*
½ cupful milk

Mix together the nuts, breadcrumbs, onion and seasoning. Beat the eggs with the *Marmite* (or *Vecon*) and milk and then combine all the ingredients. Set the mixture aside for half an hour, then place it in a greased ovenproof dish and steam it for 2 hours, or bake it for 1 hour at 300°F/150°C (Gas Mark 2), standing the dish in water. Serve hot or cold or fried in slices.

Rissole Nut Mix II

1 cupful ground peanuts
1 cupful ground walnuts
1 large onion, grated
1 teaspoonful wholemeal flour
3 large tomatoes
1 egg, beaten
1 thick slice wholemeal bread
Sea salt and freshly ground black pepper

Boil the tomatoes in a little water. Mix together the peanuts and walnuts, crumble the bread, and add them with the onion to the tomatoes. Stir in the flour and the egg and mix well. Steam the mixture in a well greased dish for 2 hours. When cool, turn out the loaf carefully, slice it and serve with fried onions, or add it to vegetable stews. This may also be used as a sandwich filling.

BREADS

CHAPATTIS

1 lb (½ kilo) wholemeal flour
Approx. ½ pint (¼ litre) water
A little sea salt
1 teaspoonful ghee

1. Put ½ cupful of flour to one side. Mix the remaining salt and flour thoroughly.

2. Make a hollow in the centre of the flour and add the water gradually, working it in well until the water is absorbed and the dough elastic.

3. Knead the dough well for about 5 minutes, then set it aside and cover it with a damp piece of muslin for 30 minutes or more.

4. Knead lightly once more, then break off pieces of dough and shape them into small balls.

5. Dust each one with a little of the extra flour and roll it out very thinly.

6. Heat a frying pan, add the ghee, place the *chapatti* in it and when the first bubbles rise in the flour, turn the *chapatti*, using a spatula or by hand. After about 30 seconds, press down the edges and gently rotate the disc.

7. Lift the *chapatti* with a fish slice and hold it directly over the heat for a second or two. (The *chapatti* should swell and is then ready to serve. These are tricky to make at first, but once you have got the knack they can be made easily and quickly).

Note: In India, a shallow iron pan called a *tawa*, *tava* or *taoa* with a slightly concave bottom is used, which allows the *chapatti* to be moved easily. *Tawas* are available in many Indian food stores, but if you do not already have one, a thick iron frying pan will do.

PARATHAS

Until one becomes accustomed to eating them, *chapattis* are usually too dry for Western tastes, whereas *parathas* may be more palatable.

½ lb (¼ kilo) wholemeal flour
½ pint (¼ litre) water (or milk and water)
Sea salt to taste
Ghee or vegetable fat

1. Mix the dough as for *chapattis* (page 28), then knead and shape it into little balls. Cover them with a damp cloth and leave them overnight.

2. Roll each ball into a small circle, brush with a little fat and fold it over to make a semi-circle. Brush again with fat, fold and repeat the process two or three times.

3. Roll the balls of dough out into pancakes of about 7 in. in diameter.

4. Place a little fat in a heated frying pan and cook the pancake until pale brown; then turn it over and cook the other side.

POOREES

Indian cuisine sometimes bewilders the foreigner as the same dishes are often called by different names in different parts of the country. One is the *loochee* of Bengal, which is known as *pooree* almost everywhere else.

1 lb (½ kilo) fine-milled wholemeal flour
1 lb (½ kilo) ghee or vegetable fat

1. Place the flour on a board and work in ½ oz (15g) of the fat.

2. Add sufficient water to form a soft dough.

3. Divide the dough into about 36 balls and gently press each one between the palms of the hands to give an ovoid shape.

4. Sprinkle each ball with a little flour and roll it out into a circular disc about 4 in. in diameter.

5. Melt the fat in a thick-bottomed iron pan and, when hot, place a disc in it and press it with a perforated ladle. Press down the edges and then fry the other side. (If the heat is too great, remove the pan from the stove and continue to fry until the *pooree* is done).

Note: Poorees are usually eaten as a snack, with a little salt or with fried potatoes.

NIMKIS

½lb (¼ kilo) fine-milled wholemeal flour
1 teaspoonful black cummin seeds
½ teaspoonful caraway seeds
½lb (¼ kilo) ghee
Juice of ½ lemon
Sea salt to taste

1. Mix the flour with the fat, juice and seeds and add enough water to form a dough.

2. Knead well and shape the dough into about 30 small balls.

3. Roll them out very thinly and fry them in deep vegetable fat.

Note: Nimkis should be served whilst still crisp and hot.

PAROTAS

These should not be confused with *parathas.*

1lb (½ kilo) fine-milled wholemeal flour
4oz (100g) ghee or vegetable fat

1. Knead a little of the fat into the flour. (This will be much drier than the dough for *nimkis*).

2. Divide the dough into about 20 balls. Roll each one into a circular disc, fold it into a semi-circle and roll it out again.

3. Melt the remaining ghee in a shallow pan and fry the *parotas* until cooked.

Note: These are usually eaten with well seasoned curries, or with cereals such as lentils or peas.

SALT GAJA

1 lb (½ kilo) wholemeal flour
1 teaspoonful baking powder
1 lb (½ kilo) ghee or vegetable fat
Sea salt to taste
Juice of 1 lime or lemon

1. Work 2 oz (50g) of the fat into the flour, then add the lemon
    or lime juice and mix again.

2. Add the salt and the baking powder and, if necessary, a little
    water. Knead well and roll the dough into a ball.

3. Divide the ball of dough into two. Roll each half out to a
    thickness of ½ in. and make incisions on the surface with a
    pointed knife or prick the dough with a fork.

4. Cut each piece into 1 in. squares, place as many as you can in
    the heated fat and fry them.

Note: As each piece is fairly thick, the surface might cook before
the middle is quite done. So, from time to time, take the pan off
the heat and let the *gaja* bubble gently. (Cook on both sides).
Serve the *gaja* crisp and hot with a little pickle; they should have
a sweet-and-sour taste.

KHASTA

4 oz (100g) *basoon* (pea flour)
1 lb (½ kilo) fine-milled wholemeal flour
Pinch of ginger
Ghee or vegetable fat
1 teaspoonful *panch phora*

1. Place the flour in a bowl and work in 2 oz (50g) of ghee or vegetable fat.

2. Add a little water to make a dough, then shape it into balls the size of marbles, and make a dent in the middle of each one with the thumb.

3. Fry the *khasta* in deep fat at a constant heat so that the dough is cooked through.

4. Transfer the *khasta* to a dish or plate or place them in a wire sieve until all the fat has drained away.

Note: These should be crisper than *poorees* and are best served hot with ginger pieces.

SAMOSAS

These can be served as a meal in themselves or as an accompaniment to a meal. When properly made they are delicious.

1 cupful wholemeal flour
¼ cupful warm water
2 teaspoonsful ghee or vegetable oil
Vegetable fat for deep frying

For filling:
¼ small cauliflower
4 oz (100g) peas
1 small carrot, chopped
1 dessertspoonful ghee or vegetable fat
¼ teaspoonful cummin seeds
Pinch of asafoetida
¼ teaspoonful each ground ginger, chilli, allspice,
   cinnamon, cummin and coriander
1 small onion, sliced
1 clove garlic, crushed
Sea salt

1. Mix the 2 teaspoonsful of ghee into the flour, then slowly add the warm water. Mix thoroughly and knead into a soft dough.

2. Shape the dough into balls the size of walnuts and roll them out into circles of about 3-4 in. in diameter.

3. Cut each circle in half and form a cone shape. Add the filling (see below) and seal the edges in folds so that the finished *samosa* is fan-shaped. (The edges must be sealed otherwise they will break during frying).

4. Fry in deep fat until golden brown. Tap each *samosa* lightly with a teaspoon; if done, the cone will make a hollow sound.

To prepare the filling:

1. Chop the cauliflower into small pieces.

2. Heat the fat, add the cummin seeds and brown them gently.

3. Gradually add the remaining ingredients and cook until the vegetables are soft. Mash them into a paste and use it to fill the cones.

Note: Any other vegetables may be added to this filling, but they must be cut up into small pieces and then mashed. A dessert-spoonful of rissole nut mix (page 26) or ground peanuts are a tasty variation. *Samosas* may be eaten as snacks, but if prepared with a lentil or protein filling, they do make a good meal.

KACHOWRIES

1 cupful *urud dhall* (lentils)
2 cupsful fine-milled wholemeal flour
½ teaspoonful coriander
Ghee or vegetable fat for deep frying
½ teaspoonful chilli
½ teaspoonful cummin
Sea salt to taste
2 teaspoonsful ghee or vegetable fat

1. Soak the lentils overnight, then drain them, leaving only a little water.

2. Mash the lentils into a smooth thick paste, mixing in the salt and spices. (A clove of crushed garlic will enhance the flavour).

3. Combine the flour and 2 teaspoonsful of fat with a little water to make a dough. Place it under a damp cloth for an hour or more.

4. Shape pieces of dough about the size of a marble and roll them out into discs about 2½ in. wide.

5. Place some of the lentil and spice mixture in the middle of each disc and fold it into a semi-circle, taking care to seal the edges. (This can be done by pressing the end of a fork into the dough).

6. Fry the *kachowries* in deep fat, then drain them and serve hot.

PAKORAS

Basoon or pea flour is used in many recipes and imparts a flavour different from that of wheat or rice flour. It also cooks through more rapidly.

1 cupful *basoon*
1 teaspoonful each cummin seeds and baking powder
1½ teaspoonsful coriander
½ teaspoonful each allspice, cinnamon and sea salt
1 clove garlic
¼ teaspoonful dried red chilli
1 small onion
Ghee or vegetable oil for frying

1. Chop the onion and garlic finely and mash them.

2. Add the remaining ingredients and mix them well, then add water in small quantities, mixing thoroughly to break up any lumps.

3. Heat the fat, then take a teaspoonful of the mixture and drop it into the pan. The mixture should rise quickly into a ball; then turn the *pakora* and brown the other side. (Tap with a teaspoon and if it sounds hollow, it is done).

4. Lift out with a fish slice or perforated spoon, drain and serve them hot.

Note: The imaginative cook can use a variety of fillings for *kachowries* and *pakoras:* peas, string beans, pieces of cauliflower, carrots, potatoes, red and green peppers, parsley, courgettes, cucumbers, chopped dandelion and nasturtium, etc. Only a little of the mixture should be used and it must be chopped or mashed finely.

BAKI ROTI

1 lb 5 oz (650g) wholemeal flour
1 teaspoonful sea salt
2 eggs
Ghee or vegetable fat
Water to mix

1.   Sieve the flour. Add the eggs and mix them in well.

2.   Add the water gradually and when it takes on the consistency of a thick paste, knead it.

3.   Divide the dough into six, roll each portion out very thinly and spread it with the fat.

4.   Fold the pastry over, knead it again and roll it out thinly. Repeat the process.

5.   Roll out each portion to about ⅛ in. thickness, cut it into rounds and toss them into a hot, greased frying pan. Cook until the flour rises in the middle, then turn them over and cook the other side.

Note: These are best served on a warmed plate with pickle, chutney or *bhurtas* (page 104).

PILAUS

The pilau, pulao or pilaf is a dish with a rice base which is common throughout the Middle and Far East. It was taken to North Africa by the conquering Arabs who introduced it into Spain in the form of paella and into Italy as risotto; the Moguls took it to India, though it may have been there before their arrival. Few people dislike pilau which, when properly made, is delicious. The idea that pilau is fattening is mistaken, for the proportion of fat to that of rice and other ingredients need not concern even the most avid slimmer.

MUNG BEAN PILAU

1 cupful brown rice
4 oz (100g) sprouted mung beans
½ cupful ghee or vegetable fat
2 cupsful water
1 teaspoonful each *garam massala* and *panch phora*
1 onion, chopped
½ teaspoonful ground cummin
Pinch each of chilli, ginger, freshly ground black pepper
¼ teaspoonful turmeric
4 cloves garlic, crushed
Sea salt to taste
Parsley to garnish

1. Fry the rice in half the fat until golden. Fry the sprouts separately in the remaining fat.

2. Add the spices and seasoning to the rice, pour in the water and bring it to the boil, then simmer until the grains of rice are soft but still firm. (If cooked in a saucepan with a close-fitting lid, the rice should be cooked through by the time all the water has evaporated).

3. Mix the sprouted beans into the rice and decorate with the chopped parsley.

Note: Beans supply the protein in this dish, rice contains carbohydrates and fat, vitamins are supplied by the spices, and minerals by all the ingredients; in this way, mung bean pilau forms a very well balanced meal.

SIMPLE PILAU

1 carrot
4 oz (100g) peas
½ lb (¼ kilo) brown rice
1 onion
6 almonds, blanched and sliced
2 oz (50g) sultanas or raisins
12 peppercorns
Seeds of 3 cardamoms
4-6 cloves
1 blade mace
2 half-inch pieces of cinnamon
2 oz (50g) ghee or vegetable fat
Sea salt to taste

1. Melt the ghee in a saucepan and, when hot, add the rice and fry it until golden.

2. Add the salt, spices and seasonings and sufficient water to cover the rice. (Use a pan with a tight-fitting lid).

3. Slice and fry the onions and set them aside.

4. Dice the carrot finely and, if fresh peas are used, boil them with the carrots until tender but not mushy.

5. Bring the rice to the boil, then lower the heat and simmer it. When the rice is cooked through, add the raisins, carrots and peas.

6. Remove the pan from the heat 5 minutes before serving, making sure that no water remains.

Note: Serve this dish hot, garnished with fried onions, lime pickle or *brinjal* pickle and yogurt.

EGG PILAU

6 onions
4 eggs
8 tablespoonsful brown rice
½ lb (¼ kilo) ghee or vegetable fat
10 peppercorns
5 or 6 green beans
4 blades mace
10 cloves
Seeds of 10 cardamoms
1 in. piece of ginger
10-12 curry leaves
6 cloves garlic

1. Boil the eggs until hard; shell them, slice them into halves and set them aside.

2. Fry 4 of the sliced onions with the peppercorns, green beans, cloves, cardamoms, ginger and curry leaves for 2 minutes.

3. Place the rice in a saucepan with a close-fitting lid. Add the onions and spices and just cover them with water.

4. Bring the water to the boil and then simmer until the rice is cooked. (If more water is needed, add some from time to time).

5. Remove the pan from the heat and set it aside with the lid on.

6. Fry the remaining onions and garlic in a little vegetable fat until brown.

7. Place the rice, spices and vegetables on a large flat dish and garnish with the fried onions, garlic and a little chopped parsley. Serve with yogurt and sweet chutney.

Note: Remove the curry leaves before serving.

CAULIFLOWER AND MUSHROOM PILAU

2 cupsful brown rice
2 onions, sliced
4 oz (100g) mushrooms, sliced
8-10 sprigs of cauliflower
Seeds of 4 cardamoms
2 one-inch pieces cinnamon
8 cloves garlic, chopped
5 oz (125g) yogurt
1 in. piece of ginger
1 green chilli, chopped
1 teaspoonful each paprika, sea salt, cummin seeds,
  panch phora
2 tablespoonsful ghee

1. *Sauté* the mushrooms in the ghee, then add the cauliflower and fry it for a couple of minutes.

2. Drain off the fat and fry the onions and garlic.

3. Place the cardamom seeds, cinnamon, cloves and rice in a pan with the onions, garlic and fat and fry until the rice is golden brown.

4. Add the cauliflower, mushrooms, ginger, chilli, paprika, cummin seeds and *panch phora* and fry for 3 minutes.

5. Stir in the yogurt and 4 cupsful of boiling water. Bring to the boil and simmer until the rice is cooked through.

6. Remove the pan from the heat, but keep the lid on for 5 minutes. Turn the *pilau* onto a large flat dish, garnish with chopped parsley and serve with pickle.

PLAIN PILAU

2 cupsful brown rice
½ lb (¼ kilo) peas
4 oz (100g) ghee or vegetable fat
1 teaspoonful each *panch phora*, sea salt, and cummin
2-3 slices green pepper
4 cloves garlic, chopped
¼ teaspoonful each chilli powder, grated ginger, turmeric
2-3 slices red pepper
1 onion, sliced

1. Fry the rice in 3 oz (75g) of the fat and cook the peas in the remaining fat until soft.

2. Place the rice in a pan with a close-fitting lid, add the *panch phora*, salt, garlic, cummin, chilli, ginger, turmeric and red and green pepper slices.

3. Cover the rice with water, bring to the boil, then simmer until the rice is cooked through. (Do not allow the rice to stick. If more water is needed, add boiling water.)

4. Fry the sliced onion until brown.

5. Turn the rice out onto a large flat dish, garnish with fried onion and parsley and serve with yogurt and pickle or chutney.

MUTTER PILAU (with peas)

½ lb (¼ kilo) brown rice
4 oz (100g) ghee or vegetable fat
½ teaspoonful sea salt
Seeds of 5 cardamoms
5 one-inch sticks of cinnamon
1½ lb (¾ kilo) fresh peas
2 onions, finely sliced
5 black peppercorns
5 cloves
Sea salt to taste
1 tomato to garnish

1. Fry the onions until golden brown in the fat; add the cardamoms, cinnamon, peppercorns and cloves and brown them.

2. Add the rice and fry it for 10 minutes. Pour 2 pints (1 litre) of boiling water into the pan, add the peas, and cook until the rice is tender and the water has evaporated.

3. Turn the rice out into a dish and garnish it with thin slices of tomato. Serve with pickle, chutney and yogurt.

Variation:
Broad beans or sweet corn may be used instead of peas.

SPINACH AND AUGERGINE PILAU
(Nettles may be used instead of spinach)

Few regard the common stinging nettle *(Urtica dioica)* as an edible plant. Each spring I make myself an infusion of nettles, draining off the water for use in a soup, and chopping up the tender nettle tops; these are then spread with butter and topped with a poached egg. The taste is very much like that of spinach. Nettles can be added to numerous other dishes such as pies and casseroles, and they also help to make excellent compost. For use in cooking, nettles should be collected from hedges bordering fields or from any area not contaminated by petrol fumes.

¾ lb (350g) brown rice
4 oz (100g) ghee or vegetable fat
Sprig each of coriander leaves and parsley
4 oz (100g) desiccated coconut
Seeds of 6 cardamoms
8 cloves
1 in. stick of cinnamon, splintered
1 red chilli, chopped
2 oz (50g) cashew nuts
4 oz (100g) coconut, fresh if possible
2½ oz (65g) *basoon* (pea flour)
4 onions
6 cloves garlic
¼ teaspoonful asafoetida
1 lb (½ kilo) *brinjals* (aubergines) or stinging nettles
½ green pepper
½ red pepper
2 cupsful milk
1 teaspoonful black cummin
12 peppercorns
1 egg

1. Soak the rice overnight, then drain it.

2. Heat a little butter in a pan, add the parsley, coriander leaves, desiccated or fresh coconut, half the cardamoms (bruised), the cinnamon, 2 of the onions (chopped) and the asafoetida. Brown them in the butter, then grind them to a paste with a little sea salt and water.

3. Cut the aubergines down the middle, prick them with a fork and rub in the paste.

4. Tie the aubergines together with a thread and grill them. When tender, put them to one side.

5. Chop the red and green peppers with the spinach or nettles and cook them in the milk until only about 2 tablespoonsful of liquid remains; then fry the mixture in butter.

6. Stir in the *basoon*, a little at a time, and season with sea salt, chilli and parsley. When cool, add the egg and mix the ingredients to a stiff paste.

7. Shape the mixture into walnut-sized balls, fry until crisp and then dust them with the black cummin.

8. Heat the butter, add the remaining cinnamon, cloves, peppercorns and rice and fry for 5 minutes.

9. Pour in enough water to cover the rice by at least 1 in., bring to the boil and then simmer with the aubergines and balls of spinach or nettles until the rice is cooked (about 20 minutes).

10. Fry the remaining onions and use them to garnish the pilau. Sprinkle the cashew nuts and coconut over the top and serve with pickle or chutney.

CAULIFLOWER AND CARROT PILAU

1 cupful brown rice
4 small carrots
1 cupful cauliflower florets
¾ cupful peas
2 large onions, finely sliced
¾ cupful mixed nuts, mostly almonds (blanched)
2 tablespoonsful ghee or vegetable fat
Seeds of 4 cardamoms
2 one-inch sticks of cinnamon
5 dessertspoonsful sultanas
Sea salt to taste
4-6 bay leaves
Parsley and paprika to garnish

1. Soak the rice for 1 hour. Scrub the carrots and chop into pieces.

2. Place the carrots, cauliflower and peas in a saucepan with a little water and boil them until tender but not soft. Strain the vegetables and keep the cooking liquid for stock.

3. Fry 1 onion and the nuts in a tablespoonful of the fat until golden brown, then remove the pan from the heat.

4. Place the vegetables in the remaining fat, *sauté* and mix them well, taking care not to break the cauliflower heads. Add the cardamom seeds and cinnamon. (Do not allow the vegetables to brown).

5. Drain the rice and place it in a large pan with the onions and nuts. Add the sultanas and cook the mixture gently for 2 minutes; pour in the stock and mix in the salt and bay leaves.

6. Bring the stock to the boil and simmer until the rice is tender and the stock is completely absorbed. (If the stock is absorbed before the rice is cooked, add a little water)

7. Combine the rice and vegetables, empty them into a flat dish and garnish with the remaining onions (fried crisply), and the chopped parsley and paprika. Serve with chutney or pickle.

Note: This dish is often served with a thick *dhall*.

KHICHIRI

Khichiri, from which the word 'kedgeree' is derived, is a popular meal, possibly because of its simplicity. In India, this is a vegetarian dish and although there are many kinds of *khichiri*, they basically fall into two categories – dry and wet. I much prefer the dry variety.

1 cupful each brown rice and green or red lentils
1 handful coriander leaves, chopped
4 cloves garlic, chopped
½ teaspoonful each turmeric and cummin seeds
¼ teaspoonful chilli or 1 teaspoonful paprika
1 teaspoonful *panch phora*
1 onion, finely chopped
1 carrot, diced
1 tablespoonful ghee or vegetable fat
Sea salt to taste

1. Combine the coriander, garlic, turmeric, cummin seeds, chilli (or paprika) and *panch phora*.

2. Fry the spices for 2 minutes in the fat, then add the lentils and rice. (The green lentils should be soaked overnight as they are more difficult to break up than the red variety).

3. Place the lentils and rice in a pan and cover them with water. Bring to the boil, then simmer. (Add the salt and carrots during the cooking process).

4. When the rice is cooked through, turn it out and serve with yogurt and chutney.

Variation:
Cardamom seeds may be added to the spices before cooking the rice.

PLAIN KHICHIRI

1 lb (½ kilo) brown rice
½ lb (¼ kilo) lentils
1 tablespoonful ghee or vegetable fat
½ teaspoonful cummin seeds

1. Cook the rice and lentils in 3 pints (1½ litres) of water, simmering until soft.

2. Heat the fat and add the cummin seeds. When the seeds start to pop, remove the pan from the heat and pour the fat and cummin over the rice and lentils. Serve with yogurt and mango or lemon pickle.

BHOONA KHICHIRI

Bhoona means 'fried' and is a term usually applied to meat dishes, though there are exceptions.

½lb (¼ kilo) red lentils
½lb (¼ kilo) brown rice
2 oz (50g) ghee or vegetable fat
4 oz (100g) onions, sliced
2 hard-boiled eggs
1 teaspoonful sea salt
2-3 one-inch slices green ginger
2 bay leaves
4 cloves
Seeds of 2 cardamoms
1 in. stick of cinnamon
12 black peppercorns
Parsley to garnish

1. Fry the onions in the fat until they are a rich brown, then set them aside.

2. Fry the lentils and rice in the remaining fat, stirring them well until the fat is absorbed.

3. Add the salt, ginger, bay leaves and spices and cover the ingredients with water, using a pan with a close-fitting lid. Simmer until the water has evaporated, by which time the rice should be cooked.

4. Set the rice aside for 15-20 minutes to allow the mixture to dry.

5. Remove the bay leaves and empty the *khichiri* onto a large flat dish.

6. Garnish with the fried onions and chopped parsley. Cut the eggs lengthwise and arrange them on the rice. Serve hot with pickle or chutney.

Note: If you wish to have yellow khichiri, add ½ teaspoonful of turmeric to the rice and lentils before cooking.

BAGATHED KHICHIRI

1½ cupsful brown rice
½ cupful red lentils
1 tablespoonful ghee or vegetable fat
1 teaspoonful turmeric
½ in. piece of green ginger
1 teaspoonful sea salt
2 large onions
1 teaspoonful *panch phora*
1 tablespoonful onion stalks or chives
Parsley and paprika to garnish

1. Slice the onions finely and fry half of them in a saucepan with the rice and lentils for about 5 minutes.

2. Add the salt, cover the mixture with boiling water, add the turmeric, ginger and *panch phora* and simmer very gently until the rice is cooked through and the water has evaporated.

3. Spoon the mixture onto a warm flat dish, top with fried onions, parsley and paprika. Serve with lime or *brinjal* pickle.

DHALLS

BASIC RECIPE

4 oz (100g) lentils
2 oz (50g) ghee or vegetable fat
2 cloves garlic, chopped
1 teaspoonful sea salt
½ teaspoonful each powdered red chilli and turmeric
4 or 5 cloves

1. Bring 1½ pints (¾ litre) of water to the boil and add the salt, chilli, turmeric and garlic.

2. Stir in the lentils and simmer until a thick mash is formed, with only a little liquid left. Beat or mash the lentils.

3. Place the fat and cloves in another pan, and heat and stir them for a couple of minutes.

4. Spoon the lentils into the pan, stir and cook them gently. (This should make a very thick 'soup'). Serve with boiled rice or *chapattis* (page 28) and pickle or chutney.

Note: Some people find lentils indigestible. To overcome this they should be placed in boiling water, boiled for at least 10 minutes and whisked when cool to break them up. When *dhall* needs to be ground, a blender will do the job effectively. Do not use more than 2 oz (50g) for each person as the digestive organs of the normal sedentary worker cannot easily cope with more.

DHALL CHURCHURREE

½ lb (¼ kilo) lentils
1½ onions, sliced
1 oz (25 g) ghee or vegetable fat
1 teaspoonful each sea salt and turmeric
½ teaspoonful chilli powder
2 bay leaves

1. Melt the fat and, when hot, toss in the onions and fry them until brown and crisp.

2. In another pan, add the turmeric, chilli, bay leaves and sea salt to the lentils and cover them with boiling water. Cover the pan and simmer the lentils until soft.

3. Remove the pan from the heat when all the water has evaporated. Remove the bay leaves and garnish the *dhall* with the fried onions. *Churchurree* is best served with *chapattis* (page 28) or preferably *poorees* (page 30).

DHALL CURRY

There are innumerable varieties of this one dish.

1 cupful lentils
4 teaspoonsful ground onion
¾ teaspoonful *garam massala*
2 cloves garlic, crushed
1 onion, finely sliced
1 tablespoonful ghee or vegetable fat
½ teaspoonful each cayenne pepper and ground ginger
Sea salt to taste

1. Mix the lentils with the ground onion, *garam massala*, garlic, cayenne pepper and ginger.

2. Place the mixture in a saucepan and pour in boiling water to cover by two inches.

3. Simmer until the lentils are soft and form a thick mass, then mix them to a smooth paste.

4. Heat the ghee and fry the sliced onions in a separate pan, then add the lentils and stir them until well mixed with the fried onions.

5. Allow the mixture to simmer gently for 15 minutes. Serve with *chapattis* (page 28), *poorees* (page 30) and pickle.

DHALL VADA

1 cupful red lentils
½ teaspoonful turmeric
10 pickling onions
3 tablespoonsful rice flour
1 dried red chilli
½ fresh green chilli
1 tablespoonful curry leaves
Ghee, vegetable fat or oil
Sea salt to taste

1. Soak the lentils in a little water until soft (overnight if possible). Drain off the water and grind the lentils to a paste.

2. Mix together the turmeric and dried chilli and add them to the lentils.

3. Chop the green chilli, onons and curry leaves and add them to the lentils.

4. Stir in the rice flour and salt and knead to form a pliable dough.

5. Roll out the dough thinly, cut out biscuits and fry them until brown on both sides in the fat.

Variation:
A little fenugreek may be added to the lentils to give an alternative flavour.

DHALL PEPPER WATER (Hot)

½ cupful lentils
5 or 6 dried chillies
1 teaspoonful each mustard seeds, cummin seeds and
   turmeric
1 walnut-sized ball of tamarind
1 teaspoonful freshly ground black pepper
2 cloves garlic, crushed
2 onions, sliced
A few curry leaves
Sea salt to taste

1. Soak the lentils overnight if possible, then boil them for 10 minutes in 2 cupsful of water. Strain off the liquid, reserving it for cooking.

2. Grind the chillies, mustard and cummin seeds and turmeric.

3. Extract the tamarind juice (see page 21), add salt and pour it into the lentil water. Boil for 20 minutes.

4. Heat the fat, fry the sliced onions, garlic and curry leaves, then add the lentil pepper water and simmer for 2-3 minutes. Serve with plain boiled rice and yogurt.

DHALL AND EGG CURRY

6 eggs, hard boiled
2 oz (50g) ghee or vegetable fat
2 oz (50g) onions, chopped
½ lb (¼ kilo) lentils or split peas
1 tablespoonful *garam massala*
1 teaspoonful sea salt
½ teaspoonful freshly ground black pepper

1. Soak the split peas (overnight) and lentils (for 1 hour).

2. Shell the eggs and prick them all over with a fork, rub them with a little of the *garam massala* and set them aside.

3. Heat the fat in a saucepan, and fry the eggs for 5 minutes, shaking the pan so that they do not burn.

4. Remove the eggs and in the same fat fry the remaining *garam massala* with half the onions until brown.

5. Add the drained lentils or split peas, stir and cook them for 5 minutes over a low heat, then add 1 pint (½ litre) of boiling water.

6. As soon as the water is absorbed, mix in the eggs, salt, remaining onions and another ½ pint (¼ litre) of boiling water.

7. Cover the saucepan and let the mixture simmer until all the water has been absorbed. (By this time, the lentils should be fully swollen).

8. Add the pepper and serve hot with rice and yogurt or with *poorees* (page 30) and chutney.

DHALL MASH

1 cupful *chunna dhall* (split peas)
1 onion, finely chopped
1 green chilli, chopped
1½ tablespoonsful thick coconut milk
1 teaspoonful ground ginger
1 tablespoonful ghee
3 cloves garlic
½ teaspoonful turmeric
Sea salt to taste

1. Soak the split peas overnight, then boil them in 3 cupsful of water until soft. Drain and set them aside.

2. Heat the fat, stir in the onion, ginger, garlic and turmeric and fry for 2-3 minutes.

3. Add the salt, *dhall* and green chilli, stir well and mash the mixture and then simmer it for 5 minutes.

4. Before removing the pan from the heat, stir in the thick coconut milk (page 21). The mash should be thick and is usually eaten with *parathas* (page 29) and pickle or chutney.

DHALL WITH SPINACH OR NETTLES

1 cupful lentils
1 lb (½ kilo) spinach or nettles, chopped
1 onion, sliced
4 cloves garlic, chopped
1 teaspoonful each coriander, turmeric and cummin seeds
½ teaspoonful chilli
½ in. piece of green ginger
Sea salt to taste
Juice of 1 lemon
Ghee or vegetable fat for frying

1. Boil the lentils until soft.

2. Heat 1 dessertspoonful of fat and fry the onion, garlic, coriander, turmeric, cummin and chilli for 3 minutes, then add the lentils, ginger and chopped spinach (or nettles).

3. Bring to the boil and then simmer for 10-15 minutes.

4. Add the salt and lemon juice and serve with rice or *chapattis* (page 28) and pickle.

Note: If nettles are used, pick only the tender top leaves during the first month of growth. Nettles are rich in iron, sulphur, sodium and vitamin C and are a much undervalued herb.

CALCUTTA DHALL BHATT

1 cupful lentils
¼ in. piece of green ginger
1 teaspoonful turmeric
1 dessertspoonful ghee or vegetable fat
2 onions, sliced
4 cloves garlic, chopped
½ green chilli, chopped
Sea salt to taste

1. Place the lentils in boiling water and simmer until soft.

2. Fry the onions, garlic, ginger and chilli for 2 minutes, then add the lentils and turmeric. Beat well to ensure that the lentils are broken up completely and that the mixture is fairly thick but not solid.

3. Place the *dhall* on a bed of rice and serve with hot pickle or chutney and yogurt. (This simple dish is a great favourite throughout Bengal).

DHALL CHUTNEY

1 cupful lentils
3 onions, chopped
3 tablespoonsful coconut milk
6 green chillies, chopped
2 cloves garlic, chopped
Juice of 1 lemon or lime

1.   Bring 3 cupsful of water to the boil, then add the lentils.

2.   Add 2 onions, the chillies and garlic.

3.   When the lentils are soft, drain them and keep the water for stock or pepper water (page 24).

4.   Mash the lentils to a thick paste and mix in the coconut milk.

5.   Fry the remaining onion, stir it into the lentils and add the lime or lemon juice.

DHALL FRITTERS

½ lb (¼ kilo) lentils
4 onions, sliced
1 egg
1 teaspoonful each cummin and turmeric
Seeds of 2 cardamoms
2 cloves garlic, crushed
1 cupful natural yogurt
1 dried red chilli, crushed
½ green chilli, sliced
Sea salt to taste
Vegetable fat for frying

1. Cover the lentils with water and soak them overnight.

2. Drain and grind them, mixing in all the ingredients to make a thick batter.

3. Drop teaspoonsful of the batter into the hot vegetable fat, which should be deep enough to cover the fritters.

4. Remove the fritters when they have risen to the surface and are cooked (1-2 minutes).

Variation:
½ teaspoonful of cinnamon may be used instead of cardamom.

GENERAL CURRIES

BRINJAL AND TOMATO CURRY

1 *brinjal* (aubergine), diced
1 tablespoonful ghee or vegetable fat
3 tomatoes, chopped
½ teaspoonful cummin
¼ teaspoonful chilli
1 teaspoonful turmeric
1 red pepper, chopped
½ teaspoonful asafoetida
1 onion, sliced
Sea salt to taste

1. Fry the pepper in the fat until tender, then set it aside. Do the same with the *brinjal*.

2. Fry the onion until golden brown, add the tomatoes and mix in the turmeric, pepper, cummin, chilli, asafoetida and salt.

3. Stir well and cook the mixture for 5 minutes at a moderate heat. Add the *brinjal*, mix and cook gently for 5 minutes. Serve the curry with rice and pickles.

Note: One advantage of the *brinjal* over many vegetables is that it cooks through rapidly; such dishes can therefore be prepared quickly.

BRINJAL AND NUTMEAT BAKE

2 large *brinjals* (aubergines)
2 eggs
6-8 tablespoonsful rissole nut mix (page 26)
2 onions, finely sliced
2 teaspoonsful *garam massala*
2 egg whites
3 small onions, chopped
Wholemeal breadcrumbs
Sea salt to taste
Ghee or vegetable fat

1. Cut off the stalk ends of the *brinjals*. With a grapefruit knife, scoop out the flesh and mash it with the onions and rissole nut mix.

2. Semi-boil the eggs so that the yolks are still soft. Mash them into the *brinjal* mixture.

3. *Sauté* the remaining onions until golden brown, stir in the *garam massala* and cook over a high heat for 2 minutes.

4. Mix this into the *brinjal* mixture and add salt to taste.

5. Whisk the egg whites and stir in the breadcrumbs.

6. Stuff the *brinjals* with the rissole nut mix, roll them in the breadcrumbs, fix on the stalk ends and bake them at 350°F/180°C (Gas Mark 4) for 30 minutes. Serve with rice, chutney and pickle.

Note: Garlic may be added to the rissole nut mix to enhance the flavour.

BRINJAL CURRY

2 *brinjals* (aubergines)
1 tablespoonful each coriander and ghee or vegetable oil
3 cloves garlic
½ teaspoonful cummin
1 dried red chilli
¼ coconut or dessicated coconut
1 green chilli, chopped
4 half-inch pieces of ginger
2 tablespoonsful cider vinegar
10 pickling onions
1 teaspoonful each turmeric and mustard seeds
3-4 curry leaves
Sea salt to taste

1. Cut the *brinjals* into ¼ in. slices. Mix the turmeric with a little salt and water to form a fine paste.

2. Prick the slices with a fork and rub in the paste on both sides.

3. Grind together the coriander, cummin, dried chilli and garlic.

4. Extract the milk from the coconut (see page 21).

5. Heat the fat in a saucepan. Slice 4 onions and *sauté* them with the curry leaves and mustard seed.

6. When the onions are brown, add the ground spices and the second and third extracts of coconut milk. Mix the ingredients well, bring to the boil, then simmer.

7. Add the green chilli, ginger, remaining onions and vinegar. (Stir well as you pour in the vinegar; this will prevent any curdling). Add the thick coconut milk.

8. Fry the *brinjal* slices until brown on each side. Cook them gently in the curry for a few minutes and season to taste with a little salt. (The *brinjals* should sink into the gravy and coconut milk). Serve at once with rice, yogurt and *dhall*.

BRINJALS WITH YOGURT

2 large *brinjals* (aubergines)
1 onion, sliced
1 small carton yogurt
1 dried red chilli, chopped
1 teaspoonful each mustard seeds and *garam massala*
4 cloves garlic, chopped
1 tablespoonful lemon juice
1 teaspoonsful each sage and thyme, chopped
Ghee or vegetable fat
Sea salt to taste
Parsley and chives to garnish

1. Boil the *brinjals* until tender. When cooked, chop them into small pieces (with the skin on) and then mash them.

2. Heat the fat, add the mustard seeds and stir them until they pop.

3. Stir in the onion, garlic, *garam massala* and dried chilli and fry them.

4. Add the yogurt and mix it in well. Stir in the *brinjal*, sage and thyme and mix well, adding a little water if necessary.

5. Sprinkle the mixture with lemon juice and serve hot on a bed of rice. Garnish with chopped parsley and chives.

STUFFED BRINJALS

2 large *brinjals* (aubergines)
1 green chilli, chopped
¼ teaspoonful black pepper
4 oz (100g) rissole nut mix (page 26)
1 large onion, finely chopped
½ in. piece of green ginger
1 tablespoonful wholemeal breadcrumbs
1 dessertsponful ghee or vegetable fat
Sea salt to taste

1. Boil the *brinjals* until tender. When cool, cut them in half, scoop out the pulp and set it aside.

2. Heat the fat and brown the onion with the ginger and chilli.

3. Fry the *brinjal* pulp separately, add the ginger, onion and chilli, mix in the rissole nut mix and season with the salt and pepper.

4. Stuff the mixture into the scooped out halves, roll them in a thick layer of breadcrumbs and bake gently until the outsides of the *brinjals* are cooked through. Serve with rice, yogurt and pickle or chutney.

POTATO FRITTERS

½ lb (¼ kilo) potatoes
1 tablespoonful fine-milled wholemeal flour
Dash of freshly ground black pepper
1 teaspoonful *panch phora*
2 cloves garlic, crushed
2 eggs
½ green chilli, sliced
½ lb (¼ kilo) onions, sliced
Sea salt to taste
Vegetable fat for frying

1. If the potatoes are new, scrub them rather than peel them.

2. Grate the potatoes and mix them with the onions.

3. Beat the eggs with enough flour to make a thick batter.

4. Mix in the pepper, *panch phora*, chilli, garlic and salt, and add the potato and onion.

5. Drop spoonsful of the mixture into hot vegetable fat, making sure the fritters are immersed. When cooked, remove and drain them, and serve with rice and a little pickle or chutney.

TOOKA

These are potatoes fried in the Indian way – a variation on chips.

2 large potatoes
½ teaspoonful each chilli powder, cummin and coriander
½ cupful peanut oil or vegetable fat
Sea salt to taste

1. Scrub the potatoes to remove all blemishes. (Peel them only if the skins are tough and rough).

2. Cut the potatoes into ½ in. slices, bring the fat to the boil and slip the slices in.

3. When the potatoes are half-fried, remove and drain them. Place them on a board and press them until they are half the thickness.

4. Add the salt, chilli, coriander and cummin to the fat. Mix and fry the spices for 2 minutes, then fry the potato slices until they are golden brown. Serve hot with steamed green beans and carrots.

POTATO CAKES

1 large or 3 medium-sized potatoes
6 tablespoonsful rissole nut mix (page 26)
1 teaspoonful freshly ground black pepper
1 green chilli, chopped
1 large sprig parsley, chopped
1 teaspoonful sage
Vegetable fat for frying
Wholemeal flour and breadcrumbs
1 egg, beaten
1 teaspoonful each cummin and *panch phora*
½ teaspoonful turmeric
1 tablespoonful tomato *purée*
Juice of 1 lemon
Sea salt to taste

1. Place the rissole nut mix in a bowl. Add the herbs, spices, lemon juice and tomato *purée* and mix thoroughly. (If too thick, add a little water or extra *purée* or both).

2. Boil the potato until it is soft enough to be mashed. Add a little fat to form a thick mixture.

3. Take 1 dessertspoonful of potato, flatten it, place some rissole nut mix on it, and cover with another layer of potato.

4. Seal the edges, sprinkle the cakes lightly with flour, brush them with the egg and coat them with the breadcrumbs.

5. Fry each one in the fat, sprinkle with chopped parsley and serve with steamed carrots, parsnips and chutney.

MANGO CURRY

6 green mangoes
1 teaspoonful each mustard, fenugreek and cummin seeds
2 tablespoonsful ghee
5 dried red chillies
½ teaspoonful each turmeric and mustard
Sea salt to taste
A few curry leaves

1. Pare and slice the mangoes thinly, discarding the stones.

2. Fry the teaspoonful of mustard, fenugreek, chillies and cummin and pound the mixture in a mortar while still warm.

3. Add the turmeric and pound again.

4. Melt the fat in a pan, stir in the curry leaves and the remaining mustard, then add the powdered and pounded spices and mix well.

5. Add the mango and cook for 10 minutes, stirring constantly.

6. Cover with water and simmer until the mixture is thick.

7. Season to taste, then serve this curry with plain boiled rice and yogurt.

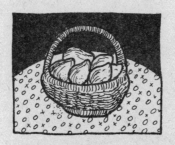

BANANA SKIN CURRY

2 cupsful green banana skin
2 tablespoonsful grated coconut
3 onions, chopped
1 heaped teaspoonful *garam massala*
1 in. piece of green ginger
3 cloves garlic, chopped
1 green chilli, chopped
1 dessertspoonful ghee
2 or 3 curry leaves
Pinch of asafoetida
Sea salt to taste

1. Wash the bananas and peel off the top green skin. Chop up 2 cupsful of the skin and cover it with water.

2. Add the salt, bring to the boil and simmer for a few minutes.

3. Heat the fat and *sauté* the onions, garlic and remaining spices.

4. Add the coconut and banana skin and simmer the mixture for 2-3 minutes. Serve hot with rice and yogurt.

Recipe taken from *The Complete Book of Curries* by Harvey Day, courtesy of the publishers Kaye and Ward Ltd.

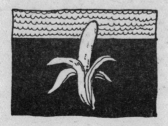

BANANA PACHADI

4 green bananas
2 onions, sliced
2 tablespoonsful coconut milk
1 green chilli, chopped
1 teaspoonful *panch phora*
2 tablespoonsful desiccated coconut
Juice of 1 lemon
Sea salt to taste

1. Boil the bananas in a little water and mash them while still hot.

2. Mix the onions and chilli with the coconut milk and desiccated coconut and add this to the bananas.

3. Mix in the *panch phora* and salt, stir well and cook gently for 5 minutes.

4. Stir well; serve with lemon juice and plain boiled rice.

DEVILLED SWEET CORN

2 tablespoonsful vegetable fat
1½ cupsful milk
1 teaspoonful sea salt
2 tablespoonsful wholemeal flour
1 teaspoonful each paprika, turmeric and mustard seeds
½ teaspoonful cummin
1 egg, beaten
2 cupsful sweet corn
1 tablespoonful *Holbrook's* Worcester sauce or
    tamarind juice
Wholemeal breadcrumbs

1. Melt the fat and stir in the flour. Add the milk gradually, stirring constantly until the mixture is thick and creamy.

2. Combine the egg with the Worcester sauce, salt, sweet corn, paprika, turmeric and mustard seeds.

3. Combine both mixtures and place them in a buttered pie dish. Cover with the breadcrumbs and a little melted butter and bake at 350°F/180°C (Gas Mark 4) until the breadcrumbs are brown.

4. Serve this dish with wholemeal bread, *chapattis* or *poorees* (pages 28 and 30) and chutney.

Note: Fresh or tinned sweet corn may be used in this recipe, although fresh corn takes longer to cook.

SAAG BHAJJI

2 lb (1 kilo) spinach or nettle tops
1 oz (25 g) ghee or vegetable fat
1 fresh green chilli, chopped
1 teaspoonful each sea salt and turmeric
4 oz (100g) onions, sliced

1. Heat the fat in a saucepan and fry half of the onions until brown.

2. Add the greens, chilli and remaining onions. (The spinach or nettle tops should be washed and drained beforehand, but some water will remain on them. No extra water should be added).

3. Stir the mixture, put a lid on the pan and simmer for 15 minutes, by which time the greens should be cooked through.

4. Stir in the salt, simmer for another minute, then serve hot. This makes a tasty dish to be served with *poorees* (page 30) or wholemeal bread, or with rice and lentils.

COURGETTES AND PEPPERS

1 lb (½ kilo) courgettes, chopped
½ red pepper, chopped
½ green pepper, chopped
1 large onion, sliced
3 cloves garlic, chopped
1 teaspoonful each *garam massala* and *panch phora*
1 dessertspoonful ghee or fat

1. Fry the onion and garlic in the fat.

2. Add the *garam massala* and *panch phora* and fry for another 2-3 minutes. (Stir constantly to prevent the mixture from sticking).

3. Place the courgettes and peppers in a pan, cover them with water and bring to the boil.

4. Add the onions, garlic, *garam massala* and *panch phora* and simmer until the 'gravy' thickens. Serve hot with rice and chutney or pickle.

CAULIFLOWER CURRY

1 medium-sized cauliflower, finely chopped or grated
1 dessertspoonful ghee or vegetable oil
1 teaspoonful turmeric
1 teaspoonful *panch phora* (optional)
Sea salt to taste

1. Heat the fat in a frying pan or deep saucepan and add the cauliflower.

2. Sprinkle in the turmeric and *panch phora*. Cook over a medium heat, stirring constantly.

3. When the cauliflower is tender, remove the pan from the heat and serve hot with *chapattis* or *poorees* (pages 28 and 30), with or without pickle and/or yogurt.

MARROW CURRY

½ small marrow
2 onions, sliced
1 clove garlic, chopped
1 tablespoonful ghee or vegetable oil
1 teaspoonful turmeric
½ teaspoonful each cummin, coriander and chilli
¼ pint (150ml) water
Sea salt to taste

1. Cut the marrow into slices about 4 in. long and ½ in. wide, having first removed the rind and seeds.

2. Place the fat in a saucepan and, when hot, add one of the onions and fry until brown.

3. Add the turmeric, cummin, coriander and chilli, then stir in the water and the remaining onion and garlic.

4. Cook gently until the marrow is tender. Add salt to taste, stir gently and serve hot with rice and pickle or chutney.

Note: After the marrow has been added to the pan, do not put in more than ¼ pint (150ml) of water as marrow is a watery vegetable.

SHREDDED VEGETABLE CURRY

(This is a quick, tasty and easily made dish).

1 carrot
1 medium-sized potato
¼ small cabbage
1 teaspoonful *garam massala* or *panch phora*
1 onion, sliced
2 cloves garlic, chopped
Seeds of 1 cardamom
1 teaspoonful mustard seeds
½ teaspoonful turmeric (if *garam masala* is not used)
Sea salt to taste

1. Shred the cabbage finely. Slice the carrot and potato lengthwise into thin strips.

2. Fry the onion until brown, then add the mustard and as soon as the seeds start to pop, stir in the *panch phora* (or *garam massala*), garlic, turmeric and cardamom.

3. Cook over a medium heat, stirring with a wooden spoon or spatula. After 8-10 minutes the vegetables should be tender but still crisp. (Do not overcook them or the cabbage will become soggy). Serve with rice, *chapattis* or *poorees* (pages 28 and 30).

Note: Other root vegetables, such as turnip or parsnip may be used instead of carrot, potato and cabbage. Runner beans are particularly suitable for this recipe.

CUCUMBER CURRY

4 cucumbers (use cucumbers that are turning yellow)
1 egg, beaten
1 green chilli, chopped
2 tablespoonsful rissole nut mix (page 26)
2 teaspoonsful *garam massala*
1 dessertspoonful cider vinegar
1 slice wholemeal bread
Pinch of ginger
4 cloves garlic, crushed
1 cupful coconut milk (page 21)
Left-over boiled potato
Sea salt to taste
A little milk

1. Soak the bread in the milk. Mash the boiled potato.

2. Peel the cucumbers and cut them into quarters.

3. Hollow out the cucumbers and mix the soft insides with the egg, chilli, *garam massala*, salt, ginger and garlic.

4. Add the bread and combine the ingredients with the nut mix to form a thick paste.

5. Place the mixture inside the pieces of cucumber and cover them with any remaining mixture.

6. Place the cucumber in a saucepan, pour in the coconut milk and simmer gently until the rissole nut mix has cooked through. Serve with boiled rice, garnished with parsley and grated carrot, chutney or pickle.

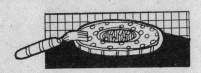

CURRIED VEGETABLE LOAF

2 cupsful carrot, cooked and diced
1 cupful string beans, cooked
2 cupsful left-over potatoes, sliced
1 onion, chopped
1 cupful wholemeal breadcrumbs
2 eggs, beaten
½ teaspoonful grated nutmeg
4 tablespoonsful ghee or vegetable fat
3 tablespoonsful wholemeal flour
½ pint (¼ litre) milk
1 teaspoonful sea salt
½ teaspoonful each chilli and cummin
1 cupful grated cheese
2 bay leaves

1. Melt the fat and stir in the flour, onion, milk, nutmeg, salt, chilli and cummin.

2. Cook until the mixture thickens, then fold in the cheese. Remove from the heat and stir in the eggs.

3. Arrange the beans, potatoes and carrots in layers in a greased baking dish.

4. Pour the thick mixture of eggs, spices and cheese over the vegetables, cover with breadcrumbs and bake at 350°F/180°C (Gas Mark 4) for 30 minutes. Serve with wholemeal bread or *poorees* (page 30) and chutney.

GREENS (KERA) CURRY

2 handsful seed or bean sprouts
6 small onions, chopped
2 dried red chillies, crushed
2 or 3 curry leaves
1 cupful coconut milk (page 21)
1 dessertspoonful ghee or vegetable fat
1 teaspoonful *garam massala*
Sea salt to taste

1. Cook 4 of the onions with the *garam massala*, chillies and curry leaves.

2. Boil the sprouts in the coconut milk, then add the spices and cook until the mixture is nearly dry.

3. Place the fat in a frying pan, add the remaining onions and, when brown, add the greens and simmer for 5 minutes.

4. Remove the curry leaves and serve the greens hot on a bed of rice with yogurt and pickle or chutney.

TOMATO CURRY

12 large tomatoes, fresh or canned
1 dessertspoonful *garam massala*
3 onions
1 dessertspoonful coriander leaves
1 in. stick of cinnamon
½ coconut
½ in. piece of green ginger
3 cloves garlic
1 tablespoonful vegetable fat
Seeds of 3 cardamoms
Sea salt to taste

1. Chop the ginger, onions, coriander leaves, garlic and *garam massala*.

2. Heat the fat and stir in the coconut flesh with the tomatoes (whole if fresh).

3. Add the remaining ingredients and stir over a low heat until the mixture thickens. Serve with rice and pickle or *poorees* (page 30) and yogurt.

Note: As no water is used, this curry will keep well – without a refrigerator – for up to a week.

MIXED VEGETABLE CURRY

3 cupsful vegetable stock (or *Vecon, Marmite* or *Yeastrel*
   stock)
4 onions, thinly sliced
1 tablespoonful ghee or vegetable fat
1 green chilli, halved
¼ coconut, ground
2 teaspoonsful each *garam massala* and tamarind juice
Seeds of 4 cardamoms
3 or 4 curry leaves
4 cloves garlic, chopped
4 half-inch slivers green ginger
Seasonal vegetables
Sea salt to taste

1. Heat the fat and fry the onions, garlic, green chilli, curry
    leaves and ginger for 2 minutes.

2. Add the spices and fry for another 2 minutes.

3. Chop or dice about 3-4 cupsful of green peas, carrots, beans,
    cabbage, cauliflower or any other vegetables in season,
    using only a little of each kind.

4. Cover the vegetables with the stock, adding a little water if
    necessary. Mix in the coconut and salt to taste.

5. Boil the vegetables until tender, then stir in the tamarind
    juice a minute or two before serving.

Note: This curry should not be too watery. Remember that
Marmite, Yeastrel and *Vecon* contain a great deal of salt, as does
celery. (If you put a stick or two of celery through a juicer, you
will be amazed how salty it tastes).

BITTER VEGETABLE CURRY (KERALA CURRY)

Keralas may be bought in some shops that specialize in Indian food; they are also available canned.

2 lb (1 kilo) *keralas*
4 red chillies
5 black peppercorns
1 cupful ghee or vegetable fat
1 dessertspoonful cummin seeds
1 small clove garlic, whole
1 in. piece of green ginger
1 lb (½ kilo) small onions, sliced
2 in. piece of tamarind
Sea salt to taste

1. Mash together the ginger and garlic and extract the juice from the tamarind using cider vinegar (see page 23).

2. Cut the *keralas* into 2 in. pieces and set them aside.

3. Grind the chillies, peppercorns, turmeric and cummin seeds and mix them with the ginger, garlic and tamarind juice.

4. Heat the fat, fry the onions until they are brown, add the spices and cook for 2 more minutes.

5. Add the *kerala* pieces and half a cupful of water. Simmer for 1-2 minutes, then add the tamarind pulp. Serve with rice and a side-dish of chopped tomato, cucumber, onion and mint.

Note: If you can get *keralas* (some say *kurilla*) fresh, buy the light green ones.

STUFFED MARROW

1 small marrow
1 teaspoonful *panch phora*
1 large egg or 2 small eggs
6 tablespoonsful rissole nut mix (page 26)
1 large potato, boiled
1 onion, chopped
2 cloves garlic, chopped
2 teaspoonsful butter
Pinch of ginger
Sea salt to taste
Paprika and parsley to garnish

1. Mash the potato with the butter, *panch phora*, onion, salt, garlic and ginger.

2. Beat the egg and mix it into the rissole nut mix, then combine the potato and egg mixtures.

3. Parboil the marrow and cut it in half. Scoop out the insides, add this to the egg and potato mixture and use it to stuff the marrow.

4. Bind the two halves together and steam for 1 hour, or place the marrow in a buttered dish and bake at 350°F/180°C (Gas Mark 4) for 30 minutes.

5. Place the marrow on a bed of very finely shredded raw cabbage and garnish with paprika and chopped parsley. Serve with chutney and *poorees* (page 30).

PAPAYA CURRY

1½ cupsful papaya, chopped
½ teaspoonful each turmeric and cummin
1 tablespoonful ghee or vegetable oil
3 heaped tablespoonsful coconut
1 green chilli, chopped
4 small onions, sliced
3-4 curry leaves
1 small carton natural yogurt (optional)
Sea salt to taste

1. Place the papaya in a saucepan with the curry leaves and salt, add enough water to cover them, then bring to the boil.

2. When the fruit is parboiled, remove it from the heat.

3. Grind the coconut (fresh or desiccated) with the turmeric, cummin and chilli.

4. Brown the onions in the fat, add the remaining ingredients, simmer for 1 minute and serve with the yogurt, if preferred.

SOUR PAPAYA CURRY

Papayas, known as pawpaws in the West Indies, are a delicious fruit, often eaten at 'tiffin' (lunchtime). The fruit is cut in half, the dozens of round black seeds are easily scooped out with a spoon, and the rest is eaten as one would a melon. Papaya contains a pepsin which is an aid to digestion, and as a result, this fruit always features at banquets when it is in season. Papayas are now available in some Indian stores and within a few years, they should be as common as the brinjal and the mango.

2 cupsful papaya, chopped
2 dried chillies
¼ teaspoonful mustard
6 one-inch slices of ginger
Egg-sized ball of tamarind
5 small onions, sliced
4 cloves garlic, chopped
½ teaspoonful cummin seeds
1 green chilli, chopped
1 tablespoonful ghee or vegetable fat
3 curry leaves, chopped
Sea salt to taste

1. Grind the dried chillies, garlic, mustard and cummin seeds to a paste.

2. Extract the juice of the tamarind and add 2 cupsful of water, then mix in the spices.

3. Heat the fat in a pan and *sauté* the onions and curry leaves. When brown, add the tamarind juice and spices.

4. Stir in the papaya, green chilli and ginger and bring the mixture to the boil.

5. When the 'gravy' is thick, remove from the heat and serve hot with plain rice.

FRUIT CURRY

1 dessertspoonful cashew nuts
2 large onions
1 small papaya (pawpaw)
½ in. slice of pineapple
1 dessertspoonful desiccated coconut
1 tablespoonful coconut cream
½ teaspoonful freshly ground black pepper
1 dessertspoonful ghee or vegetable fat
1 teaspoonful each currants and sultanas
2 bananas, chopped
2 teaspoonsful *garam massala*
Juice of 1 lemon or lime
Pinch of ginger
Grated rind of ½ lemon
Sea salt to taste
Milk or whey
Cashew nuts and shallots to garnish

1. Slice the onions and fry them in the fat.

2. Stir in the *garam massala*, cook gently for 2 minutes, then add a little milk or whey to form a paste.

3. Place the onion mixture in a saucepan, add the coconut cream, desiccated coconut, ginger, currants, sultanas, bananas and lemon rind.

4. Lower the heat and cook gently for 1 hour, adding water if the mixture becomes too thick. Serve on a bed of rice and garnish with cashew nuts and chopped shallots.

Note: Papayas are sold in some Asian food shops, as is coconut cream. If papayas are not available, substitute two more slices of pineapple.

RICE CUTLETS

1 cupful brown rice
½ in. piece of green ginger
½ teaspoonful cummin
1 cupful rissole nut mix (page 26)
1 green chilli, chopped
1 teaspoonful turmeric
1 egg, beaten
Wholemeal breadcrumbs
Sea salt to taste

1. Boil the rice and drain it, then add it to the rissole nut mix.

2. Mash the ginger, add it to the cummin, chilli, salt and turmeric and combine this with the rice mixture.

3. Mould the mixture into cutlets, brush them with the egg, sprinkle them with breadcrumbs and fry until golden brown. Serve with *poorees* (page 30), pickle or chutney.

BREADFRUIT CUTLETS

This recipe was given me by Mrs Yvette Loos of Kingston, Negombo, Sri Lanka; the only difference is that, whereas she used fish, I have substituted rissole nut mix.

½ small breadfruit
4 oz (100g) onions, sliced
1 egg yolk
½ dessertspoonful chilli
1 teaspoonful turmeric
6 tablespoonsful rissole nut mix (page 26)
12 curry leaves, chopped
1 piece of rampa*
Lime or lemon juice
Wholemeal flour and breadcrumbs
Ghee or vegetable oil for frying
Sea salt to taste

1. Cut the breadfruit into large pieces, cover them with water and bring to the boil with the turmeric and salt.

2. When the breadfruit is tender, mash and mix it with the onions, rampa, curry leaves and egg yolk.

3. Remove the pan from the heat and take out the rampa. Add the rissole nut mix and mould the mixture into small cutlets.

4. Make a thin batter with a little flour and water. Dip the cutlets in the batter, roll them in the breadcrumbs and fry them in deep fat.

Note: Breadfruit is eaten in Sri Lanka, Burma, Malaysia, Indonesia and the West Indies. In India, it is eaten mainly in the South.

*Rampa is known as screw pine and is a member of the *Pandanus* species; the seeds of *Pandanus odoratissimus* are used as food, and

Pandanus houllettii yields fruit of a soft texture and a sweet pineapple flavour. Rampa adds flavour to this particular dish, but it is difficult to obtain, so may be omitted.

CURRIED BEAN SPROUTS

4 cupsful sprouted beans
1 tablespoonful vegetable fat
1 teaspoonful each grated ginger and *garam massala*
Seeds of 2 cardamoms
½ teaspoonful cummin
1 teaspoonful coriander
1 onion, sliced
2 or 3 cloves garlic, chopped
Sea salt to taste

1. Fry the onion and garlic until brown. Add the ginger, cummin, coriander, cardamom and *garam massala* and fry for 2-3 minutes.

2. Mix in the sprouts and stir them to prevent sticking; cover them with water and simmer until most of the water has evaporated. Serve on a bed of rice with pickle or chutney.

KHUTTA CURRY

1 carrot, chopped
1 medium-sized potato, chopped
3 in. piece of parsnip
4-6 artichokes
2 in. slice of marrow
4 teaspoonsful ground onions
1 teaspoonful turmeric
½ teaspoonful dried red chilli
4 cloves garlic, crushed
1 teaspoonful coriander seeds
2 in. ball of tamarind
1 teaspoonful jaggery or molasses
Sea salt to taste
Ghee or mustard oil

1. Dissolve the tamarind in boiling water. Mash, then strain it through a muslin cloth, making approximately 2 cupsful.

2. Sweeten the tamarind with the jaggery or molasses.

3. Add the strained liquid to the potato, parsnip, artichokes and marrow and simmer over a low heat.

4. Fry the onions and garlic in the ghee or mustard oil.

5. Add the turmeric, chilli and coriander seeds and brown them for 2 minutes.

6. Stir in the vegetables and tamarind water; place a lid on the saucepan and simmer until the vegetables are cooked. Serve with rice and a small dish of diced tomato, cucumber and mashed mint in a teaspoonful of cider vinegar.

Note: Yogurt also makes a good accompaniment to this curry.

EGG CURRY

4 eggs
2 oz (50g) ghee or vegetable fat
2 oz (50g) onion, chopped
¼ pint (150ml) water
1 heaped teaspoonful *garam massala*
1 teaspoonful ground ginger
2 cloves garlic, chopped
1 teaspoonful cider vinegar
A little lemon juice
Sea salt to taste
Paprika and parsley to garnish

1.   Boil the eggs for 15 minutes, then dip them in cold water for 1 minute.

2.   Remove the shells and prick the eggs all over with a fork.

3.   Make a paste using the *garam massala*, cider vinegar and sea salt and rub the paste into the eggs well.

4.   Heat the fat in a saucepan and fry half of the onion until brown.

5.   Add the eggs and cook them gently, making sure they do not stick or burn.

6.   Add the boiling water and remaining onion, cover the pan and simmer until only a thick gravy remains. Serve on a bed of rice topped with paprika and chopped parsley and chutney.

CURRY PIE

½ lb (¼ kilo) fine-milled wholemeal pastry flour
4 oz (100g) ghee or vegetable fat
2 oz (50g) broad beans
1 small carrot, chopped
1 small potato, chopped
½ small tin garden peas
2 teaspoonsful *garam massala*
1 teaspoonful *panch phora*
1 green chilli, chopped
1 large onion, sliced
4 cloves garlic, chopped
Ghee or vegetable fat for cooking
Pinch of ginger
Sea salt to taste

1. Mix the flour and fat thoroughly and add water to make a workable dough.

2. Divide the dough into two, roll out one half and use it to line a greased 7 in. baking dish.

3. Parboil the beans, carrots, potatoes and peas and reserve the cooking water.

4. Heat the fat and fry the onion for 1 minute. Add the garlic, chilli, *garam massala, panch phora* and, if you like, a sprinkling of powdered ginger. Fry for 2 minutes.

5. Add enough water to make a thick sauce (making use of the water in which the vegetables were boiled).

6. Mix the vegetables with the fried spices and spoon them onto the pastry case.

7. Roll out the other half of the dough and place it over the vegetables. Seal down the edges, using a fork, and make slits in the top to let out the steam.

8.   Bake the pie in a pre-heated oven at 300°F/150°C (Gas Mark 2) for 30 minutes.

Note: The pie mixture may be varied by using green beans, parsnips, butter beans, runner beans or any other vegetable such as chopped red and green peppers. Experiment and use your imagination!

DAHI CURRY

1½ cupful natural yogurt
½ teaspoonful each turmeric and cummin seeds
1 red chilli, crushed
1 dessertspoonful ground coconut
1½ dessertspoonsful ghee or vegetable fat
½ cupful coriander leaves
4 cloves garlic, crushed
1 cupful *basoon* (pea flour)
Seeds of 3 cardamoms
Sea salt to taste

1.   Grind the coconut (fresh or desiccated) to a pulp together with the turmeric, chilli, coriander leaves, cummin seeds and garlic.

2.   Heat the fat and stir in the yogurt, spices and *basoon*.

3.   Add the salt and simmer gently until the *basoon* is cooked through.

4.   Combine both mixtures and serve with rice and a *bhurta* of chopped cucumber, tomato, chives and mint.

CURRY CAKES

1 cupful *basoon* (pea flour)
½ cupful onions, chopped
1 green chilli, sliced
1 teaspoonful turmeric
½ teaspoonful cummin
1 egg
Seeds of 2 cardamoms
6 spring onions, chopped
¼ cupful coriander leaves, chopped
½ in. piece of green ginger
¼ coconut
Ghee or vegetable fat for cooking
Tomato *purée* or juice
Sea salt to taste

1. Mix together the spring onions, chilli, egg, turmeric, cummin, cardamom, coriander leaves, ginger, *basoon* and coconut flesh to form a thick paste.

2. Add the tomato *purée* to taste and shape the mixture into small flat cakes.

3. Heat the fat and fry a few cakes at a time. When cooked on one side, turn and cook them on the other. These make a tasty and nutritious supper snack to be served with *poorees* (page 00) and a little chutney and pickle.

CAPSICUM CURRY

3 capsicums (peppers)
1½ tablespoonsful ghee or vegetable fat
1 teaspoonful *panch phora*
Juice of 1 lime or lemon
6 dessertspoonsful rissole nut mix (page 26)
½ teaspoonful *garam massala*
¾ cupful thick coconut milk
3 cloves garlic, chopped
Seeds of 2 cardamoms
Tomato *purée* (optional)
Sea salt to taste

1. Scoop out the insides of the capsicums and set them aside.

2. Mix the rissole nut mix with a little tomato *purée* or water, *panch phora* and salt, and stuff the mixture into the capsicums.

3. Pour the coconut milk into a saucepan, add the *garam massala* and cook rapidly for 2 minutes.

4. Place the capsicums in a baking dish, pour the coconut and *garam massala* mixture over them and bake in a moderate oven at 350°F/180°C (Gas Mark 4) for 30 minutes.

5. Sprinkle the lemon or lime juice over the top and serve hot with rice and pickle or chutney.

CURRY PUFFS

For filling:
6 tablespoonsful rissole nut mix (page 26)
1 cupful shallots, finely chopped
1 teaspoonful each mustard and cummin seeds
½ teaspoonful turmeric
2 teaspoonsful coriander seeds
6 thin slices green ginger
2 tablespoonsful ghee or vegetable fat
2 egg yolks
4 oz (100g) desiccated coconut
2 small onions, sliced
1 red chilli, chopped
½ green chilli, chopped (optional)
6 cloves garlic
1 dessertspoonful lemon juice
Sea salt to taste

1. Grind together the coconut, shallots, turmeric, mustard and coriander seeds, ginger, cummin seeds, garlic, salt and chillies.

2. Add the rissole nut mix and bind the ingredients with the egg yolks.

3. *Sauté* the onions until nearly brown, then add the rissole nut mix, spices and lemon juice. (If too dry, add a little water).

4. Cook the mixture to form a fairly thick paste.

For dough:
7 oz (200g) self-raising, fine-milled wholemeal pastry flour
3½ oz (90g) ghee or vegetable fat
Approx. 6 tablespoonsful water

1. Work the fat into the flour, then add the water by degrees to form a pliable dough.

2. Roll out the dough and cut it into rounds of about 3-3½ in.

3. Place some of the curry filling on each circle, turn one half of the dough over the other and seal the edges, using a fork to make the indentations.

4. Heat a little vegetable fat in a frying pan, slide in the puffs and fry them on both sides until light brown.

5. Drain the puffs on a wire rack and serve them hot. Without any accompaniment, these make a tasty supper snack; they are filling and nutritious.

Note: Plain flour may be used instead of self-raising.

BUTTERMILK CURRY

1 pint (½ litre) buttermilk
½ teaspoonful cummin seeds
3 small onions, chopped
1 teaspoonful each mustard and fenugreek seeds
1 dessertspoonful curry leaves
2 tablespoonsful grated coconut
3 dried red chillies, chopped
1 tablespoonful ghee or vegetable oil
Sea salt to taste

1. Combine the coconut, cummin, onions and chillies to form a paste, then mix in the buttermilk.

2. Heat the fat and add the curry leaves, fenugreek and mustard seeds. As soon as the mustard stops popping, add the buttermilk mixture.

3. Add the salt and boil the mixture rapidly until it thickens. Serve with rice and a *bhurta* of cucumber, tomato, parsley and mint, chopped and mixed with 1 teaspoonful of wine vinegar.

A FEW IDEAS TO ACCOMPANY THE MEAL

SHREDDED CABBAGE

¼ small cabbage
½ teaspoonful turmeric
1 teaspoonful *panch phora*
1 onion, sliced
Ghee or vegetable fat for frying
Sea salt to taste

1. Shred the cabbage, but not too finely.

2. Heat the fat, fry the onion and add the turmeric, salt and *panch phora*. Fry over a medium heat for about 10 minutes – or less – until the cabbage is cooked through but still crisp.

3. Remove the pan from the heat and serve the cabbage either with curry and rice, or on its own with *poorees* (page 30) and pickle.

GREEN MANGO BHURTA

1 large green mango
6 fresh mint leaves
1 teaspoonful raw cane sugar
¼ teaspoonful ground red chilli
½ teaspoonful each ground ginger and sea salt
1 teaspoonful cider vinegar

1.   Peel and remove the flesh from the mango, then mash it to a pulp using a pestle and mortar.

2.   Mix the sugar with the pulp, then add the salt, ginger, chilli and mint leaves, using the vinegar to bind them. (If the mango tastes too acid, add a little more sugar).

Note: A similar *bhurta* can also be made with a cooking apple instead of mango. Of course, the flavour will be rather different, in which case a little tomato juice may be added.

BANANA SKIN SALAD

6 large bananas
4 tablespoonsful cider vinegar
1 green chilli, chopped
6 small onions, chopped
¼ ripe coconut or desiccated coconut
Sea salt to taste

1. Scrub the bananas well. Using a potato peeler or sharp knife, remove the top green or yellow skin and wash it in cold water, then boil it in lightly salted water until soft.

2. Drain the skins, chop them up and place them in a salad bowl with the onions and chilli.

3. Cover the salad with thick coconut milk (see page 21), and serve as an accompaniment to rice and curry.

Note: Be sparing in the use of coconut milk, as this salad should be thick.

FRIED BRINJALS

In France, *brinjals* or aubergines are a common vegetable and there are indeed many ways to prepare them. One of the simplest is to fry them.

2 *brinjals* (aubergines)
1 heaped teaspoonful turmeric
Vegetable fat for frying
Sea salt to taste
Lemon juice

1. Wash the *brinjals* thoroughly and cut off the stalk end.

2. Mix the turmeric with a little sea salt and lemon juice to form a stiff paste.

3. Cut the *brinjals* into slices ¼ in. thick, prick them with a fork and smear the paste into the flesh on both sides.

4. Fry the slices in the vegetable fat.

BRINJAL SALAD

2 *brinjals* (aubergines)
1 green chilli, chopped
½ tablespoonful cider vinegar
6 small onions, chopped
½ cupful thick coconut milk
Sea salt to taste

1. Boil the *brinjals* until soft, scoop out the pulp, mash it and mix in the onions, chilli, vinegar and coconut milk. (The mixture should be thick, but if too thick, add a little water.) Serve with rice and curry, or *dhall* and curry.

CUCUMBER RAITA

½ cucumber, finely chopped
¼ teaspoonful freshly ground black pepper
Seeds of 1 cardamom
½ green chilli, chopped
1 small onion, finely chopped
2 small cartons natural yogurt
A few coriander leaves, chopped
Sea salt to taste
Parsley to garnish

1. Add a little salt to the yogurt and mix thoroughly with the cucumber, black pepper, chilli, cardamom seeds and onion.

2. Garnish with the coriander leaves and parsley.

POTATO PACHELLI

2 large 'floury' potatoes
2 green chillies, chopped
1 large onion, chopped
1 in. piece of green ginger, chopped
1 cupful thick coconut milk (page 21)
1 small carton natural yogurt
Sea salt to taste

1. Boil the potatoes until cooked through but still firm.

2. Mash them and mix in the chillies (removing the seeds if you do not want the dish to be too hot).

3. Mash the ginger and add it to the potatoes with the onion, salt and coconut milk to form a thick porridge-like consistency.

4. Whisk in the yogurt with a fork.

5. Heat the mixture through well, then simmer it for a few minutes and serve hot with *poorees* (page 30).

Note: In the North, this dish would be known as a *raita*, and is usually uncooked and served as an accompaniment to curries.

COCONUT RICE

½ lb (¼ kilo) brown rice
4 small onions, chopped
½ teaspoonful turmeric
½ coconut
6 cloves
3 cloves garlic, chopped
10 black peppercorns
Seeds of 1 cardamom
Sea salt to taste

1. Scrape the coconut, mix the flesh in boiling water and press out as much coconut milk as possible. (Use desiccated coconut if fresh is not available.) Repeat the process to produce thin milk.

2. Pour the liquid into a saucepan, add the rice, and make sure that the liquid is about 2½ in. above the rice. If not, add a little water.

3. Bring the rice to the boil and add the onions, turmeric, salt, cloves, cardamom, garlic and peppercorns. (Use a pan with a close-fitting lid.)

4. Lower the heat and simmer the rice gently until the grains are cooked through but still firm. (If the liquid has evaporated before the rice is cooked, add a little more water or coconut milk.) Serve either with curry and yogurt, or pickle and chutney.

JHALL FARAZI

1 carrot, diced
1 potato, diced
1 small parsnip, diced
1 teaspoonful mustard seeds
1 large onion, chopped
2 cloves garlic, chopped
1 cupful peas
6 black peppercorns, freshly ground
½ teaspoonful chilli
1 teaspoonful cummin
Ghee or vegetable fat for cooking

1. Fry the onions lightly in the fat. Add the garlic, mustard
   seeds, cummin, pepper and chilli. Mix and fry them for 2
   minutes.

2. Add the potato, carrot, parsnip and peas and fry until the
   vegetables are tender.

CHUTNEYS AND PICKLES

Chatni is a Hindi word used to describe fruits and vegetables preserved in vinegar and spices, and pickle (the derivation of which is unknown) is used for vegetables and fruits preserved in an acid medium and cooked in oil. The main difference between the two is that chutneys usually have a sweet taste, whereas pickles have an acid base.

At formal dinners in Indian and Pakistani homes, the foreign guest is often puzzled by the number of little dishes which are placed before him, each containing ingredients which may be unfamiliar to him. They may be chutneys, pickles or *bhurtas* which are made fresh for each meal. These are made with chopped or pounded herbs, tomato, cucumber, mint, vinegar, salt, sugar and chilli, not all, of course, in the same *bhurta* (see page 104). If left over, they may be kept in the fridge for the next meal, but should not be kept any longer.

Chutneys and pickles may be kept for months in air-tight jars without deteriorating; so may pickle curries, but not for as long as pickles and chutneys. In India, where millions eat meals consisting only of rice, or rice and *dhall*, these relishes play a considerable part in the national cuisine, and plain rice with pickle, chutney or pickle-chutney often makes an appetizing and satisfying dish.

MANGO CHUTNEY

Excellent mango chutney has been on sale in Britain for years, but there is no reason why you should not make your own.

2 green mangoes
6 heaped tablespoonsful grated coconut
6 green chillies, chopped
3 small onions, chopped
A few curry leaves, chopped
Sea salt to taste

1. Pare and slice the mangoes.

2. Grind the coconut, chillies, onions and curry leaves to a paste.

3. Add the mango slices, pound, mix and serve with rice, lentils and yogurt. (This is meant for daily use and will not keep).

SWEET MANGO CHUTNEY I

3 lb (1½ kilos) green mangoes, chopped
2 lb (1 kilo) sultanas
4 oz (100g) sea salt
3 oz (75g) dried red chillies, chopped
2 lb (1 kilo) raw cane sugar
1 lb (½ kilo) almonds
1 oz (25g) green ginger, chopped
1½ oz (40g) garlic, chopped
1½ pints (¾ litre) cider vinegar

1. Combine all the ingredients, and place in the sun or in a warm spot for 5 days.

2. Bottle the chutney in air-tight jars and keep it for at least 3 months before sampling.

SWEET MANGO CHUTNEY II

3 lb (1½ kilos) green mangoes
4 oz (100g) green ginger, chopped
1 oz (25g) chilli powder
½ pint (¼ litre) cider vinegar
3 lb (1½ kilos) raw cane sugar
4 oz (100g) garlic, sliced
1 lb (½ kilo) damsons
Sea salt to taste

1. Boil the mangoes into small pieces. Remove the stones, add the sugar and simmer until the mixture has the consistency of jam.

2. Boil the damsons until they are soft enough for the stones to be removed.

3. Combine the damsons with the mango, ginger, chilli and garlic.

4. Stir in the vinegar and salt to taste.

5. Bring to the boil, then remove the pan from the heat, and when cool, bottle the chutney. Store it for at least 3 months before using.

MUSTARD LEMON CURRY

This is usually made with limes, which are far more common in India than lemons; however, either may be used.

1 heaped tablespoonful mustard
1 dessertspoonful chopped green chillies
6 tablespoonsful ghee or vegetable oil
1 dessertspoonful curry leaves
12 salted limes or lemons (see note)
1 dessertspoonful Guyana raw cane sugar
8 dried red chillies, chopped
1 whole garlic, chopped
1 dessertspoonful chopped ginger
1½ cupsful cider vinegar
1½ teaspoonsful mustard seeds
1 teaspoonful turmeric
Sea salt to taste

1. Heat the oil and stir in the mustard and curry leaves. Fry for 1 minute, then add the chillies, garlic and ginger.

2. When brown, add the mustard seed, turmeric and chillies and fry for 5 minutes.

3. Pour in the vinegar and simmer for a couple of minutes.

4. When cool, bottle the curry in air-tight jars for storing.

Note: To salt limes or lemons, slit each one three-quarters of the way through and pack with sea salt. Place them in jars and sprinkle layers of sea salt in between the fruit. Shake well and put out in the sun or in a warm place.

For everyday use, take 1 lemon, cut it into quarters, add a chopped green chilli and a little cider vinegar and serve with plain boiled rice.

HUDDA MANGO CURRY (Pickle Curry)

10 dried mangoes, sliced
4 dried red chillies, crushed
2 pinches of cummin seed
½ teaspoonful each mustard and turmeric
1 dessertspoonful each curry leaves, sliced ginger and
　chopped garlic cloves
4 green chillies, split lengthways
3 cupsful cider vinegar
4 tablespoonsful ghee or vegetable fat
Sea salt to taste

1.　Heat the fat and stir in the mustard and curry leaves, then the chillies, cummin seed and turmeric (ground to a paste).

2.　Fry the mixture for 5 minutes, then add the vinegar, dried mangoes, ginger, cloves and green chillies.

3.　Stir and simmer the mixture over a moderate heat.

4.　When half of the vinegar has evaporated, remove the pan from the heat, add the salt and spoon the pickle into jars.

Note: This mango curry keeps for weeks, and a little eaten with rice makes a tasty meal.

BRINJAL PICKLE CURRY

2 *brinjals* (aubergines)
2 cloves garlic
½ teaspoonful each turmeric and mustard seeds
½ handful curry leaves
1 wineglassful cider vinegar
4 dried chillies
¼ teaspoonful cummin seeds
¾ tablespoonful ghee or vegetable oil
Sea salt to taste

1. Cut the *brinjals* into quarters and boil them in a little water and salt. Drain off the water and place the pieces on a plate in the sun or warm spot to dry.

2. Grind the garlic, turmeric, chillies and cummin seeds to form a paste with a little vinegar.

3. Heat the oil in a saucepan and fry the mustard seeds and curry leaves for 2 minutes.

4. Stir in the ground spices and fry them for a further 2 minutes.

5. Add the *brinjal* pieces, simmer for a few minutes, then remove them from the heat. When cool, bottle the pickle in an air-tight jar. Serve in small quantities with plenty of rice or *poorees* (page 30).

GINGER CURRY (Pickle Curry)

1 cupful ginger, finely chopped
1 teaspoonful each turmeric and fenugreek
1 dessertspoonful mustard seeds
½ handful curry leaves
15 dried red chillies
3 tablespoonsful ghee or vegetable fat
1 egg-sized ball of tamarind
Sea salt to taste

1. Grind the chillies and turmeric to a paste, using a little water.

2. Heat 1 teaspoonful of the fat in a pan and fry half of the ginger until it is dry, then add the remaining fat and, when hot, stir in the fenugreek, mustard seeds and curry leaves.

3. As soon as the mustard seeds start popping, add the remaining ginger until brown.

4. Extract the juice of the tamarind (see page 21) and mix it with the chilli and turmeric paste.

5. Add 1 pint (½ litre) of water to the tamarind mixture, simmer for a few minutes and strain when cool.

6. Pour the liquid onto the cooked ginger and simmer until it thickens.

7. Skim off any froth and, when cool, spoon it into an air-tight jar where it will keep for a fortnight or more without refrigeration.

Note: This is a very pungent pickle, so serve only a little with plenty of rice, *chapattis* or *poorees* (pages 28 and 30).

LEMON CURRY (Pickle Curry)

2 cupsful chopped lemons (greenish lemons are preferable
   to fully ripe ones)
1 heaped teaspoonful each turmeric and mustard seeds
1 coffee cupful thick tamarind juice
1 teaspoonful fenugreek
15 dried red chillies
5 tablespoonsful ghee or vegetable fat
A handful of curry leaves
Sea salt to taste

1.   With a little water, make a paste of the chillies and turmeric.

2.   Mix in the tamarind juice, add 2 cupsful of water, then strain
     the mixture.

3.   Fry the lemon pieces in 1 teaspoonful vegetable oil until the
     greenish skin fades.

4.   Heat the remaining fat in a separate pan and add the
     mustard seeds, fenugreek and curry leaves.

5.   As soon as the mustard seeds start popping, pour in the
     strained 'gravy' and boil for 15 minutes (by which time the
     gravy should thicken).

6.   Combine all the ingredients and simmer for a further 5
     minutes, adding salt to taste. Serve this curry with a great
     deal of rice as it is particularly hot and a little goes a long
     way. It also goes well with *chapattis* or *poorees* (pages 28 and
     30).

MANGO CUSSOUNDEE

A *cussoundee* is a type of relish between a pickle and a curry that will keep for months in an air-tight jar. It is often eaten with rice as a complete meal. One old recipe book states: 'Peel and slice fine one hundred green mangoes...', which obviously does not suit our purposes as mangoes bought in Britain cost between 80p and £1.00 each. The following recipe is based on much smaller quantities:

5 lb (2½ kilos) mangoes
½ pint (¼ litre) cider vinegar
½ pint (¼ litre) mustard oil
2 oz (50g) garlic, sliced
3 oz (75g) turmeric
2 oz (50g) red chillies
2 oz (50g) mustard seeds
2 oz (50g) ginger, sliced
Sea salt

1. Peel and slice the mangoes, rub them with salt, set them aside for 12 hours then wipe them dry.

2. Mix together the garlic, turmeric, red chillies, mustard seeds and ginger. Pound the mixture into a paste with a little vinegar.

3. Heat the mustard oil over a moderate heat, add the mango slices and *sauté* them until soft.

4. Stir in the vinegar and bottle the relish in air-tight jars when cool.

BRINJAL CUSSOUNDEE

2 lb (1 kilo) *brinjals* (aubergines)
2 tablespoonsful mustard seeds
1 teaspoonful turmeric
10 cloves garlic, chopped
2 one-inch pieces of green ginger
Seeds of 6 cardamoms
½ in. piece of cinnamon
¼ pint (150 ml) cider vinegar
1 tablespoonful sea salt
3 oz (75 g) jaggery or molasses
5 dried red chillies
6 cloves
10 black peppercorns
2 tablespoonsful mustard oil

1. Grind the garlic, ginger and red chillies.

2. Grind and pound the cardamom seeds, cinnamon, cloves, peppercorns and mustard seeds.

3. Cut the *brinjals* into ½ in. slices, then chop them into still smaller pieces.

4. Heat the oil – if you cannot get mustard oil, sunflower oil is a good substitute. Fry the garlic, ginger and red chillies for 2-3 minutes, then add the ground cardamom, cinnamon, cloves, peppercorns and mustard seeds.

5. When the mixture is cooking gently, add the *brinjal* pieces and continue simmering until the *brinjal* is nearly cooked through.

6. Stir in the jaggery or molasses and vinegar.

7. Cook until the 'gravy' thickens and, when cool, spoon it into air-tight jars. Serve with plain boiled rice or with rice and curry.

EASY BRINJAL CUSSOUNDEE

3 lb (1½ kilos) *brinjals* (aubergines)
2 oz (50g) raw cane sugar
1 bulb of garlic, chopped
¼ pint (150ml) mustard or sunflower oil
2 oz (50g) *garam massala* or curry paste
½ lb (¼ kilo) onions, finely chopped
¼ pint (150ml) cider vinegar

1. Cut up the brinjals, rub them with salt and set them aside.

2. Heat the oil and *sauté* the onions and garlic without browning them. Add the *garam massala* or paste and cook gently.

3. Drain the *brinjals* of any juice which salting has produced. Add them to the other ingredients and cook until all the water has evaporated and the oil rises to the surface. (When cooking, stir the *brinjals* gently in order not to break up the pieces).

4. When cool, spoon the relish into air-tight jars.

This and the previous recipe were given to me by Mrs A. H. Duncan who lived in India for nearly fifty years. They are both tasty and easily made.

TOMATO CUSSOUNDEE

3 lb (1½ kilos) tomatoes, chopped
2 oz (50g) raw cane sugar
1 bulb of garlic, chopped
¼ pint (150ml) mustard or sunflower oil
2 oz (50g) *garam masala* or curry paste
½ lb (¼ kilo) onions, finely chopped
¼ pint (150ml) cider vinegar

1. Heat the oil and *sauté* the onions and garlic without browning them.

2. Add the *garam masala* or paste and cook gently.

3. Stir in the remaining ingredients and simmer until the water has evaporated and the oil rises to the surface.

4. When cool, spoon the relish into air-tight jars.

DAMSON CUSSOUNDEE

In India, plums with a distinctly tart flavour are used for this recipe. The nearest to this type of plum is the damson.

2 lb (1 kilo) damsons
2 oz (50g) ginger
2 oz (50g) raw cane sugar or jaggery
1 pint (½ litre) mustard or other vegetable oil
2 oz (50g) garlic, chopped
½ oz (15g) dried red chillies
½ oz (15g) mustard seeds
½ pint (¼ litre) cider vinegar

1. Boil the damsons until they are soft enough for the stones to be removed.

2. Sprinkle sea salt over the fruit and place it in the sun or a warm place for 2 days.

3. Grind the ginger, garlic, mustard seeds and chillies and mix them with the vinegar.

4. Heat the oil until it bubbles, then stir in the spices.

5. Add the damsons and sugar and simmer for 30 minutes. When cool, bottle the relish in air-tight jars and keep for 3 months.

Note: If you prefer it hotter, increase the amount of chilli used.